Woven Wonder

The Tradition of Indian Textiles

For Sarah Jane

I love you!

Merri

Text Copyright © AshaRani Mathur 2002

Published 2002 by
Rupa & Co
7/16, Ansari Road, Daryaganj
New Delhi 110 002

Offices at:
15 Bankim Chatterjee Street, Calcutta 700 073
135 South Malaka, Allahabad 211 001
PG Solanki Path, Lamington Road, Mumbai 400 007
36, Kutty Street, Nungambakkam, Chennai 600 034
Surya Shree, B-6, New 66, Shankara Park,
Basavangudi, Bangalore 560 004
3-5-612, Himayat Nagar, Hyderabad 500 029

ISBN 81-7167-699-5

All rights reserved.
No part of this publication may be reproduced, stored in a retrieval system,
or transmitted in any form or by any means, electronic, mechanical, photocopying,
recording or otherwise, without the prior permission of the publishers.

Book Design & Typeset by
Arrt Creations
45 Nehru Apts Kalkaji
New Delhi 110 019
arrt@vsnl.com

Printed in India by
Ajanta Offset & Packagings Ltd.

WOVEN WONDER

THE TRADITION OF INDIAN TEXTILES

AshaRani Mathur

Rupa & Co

Acknowledgements

We would like to thank the following:
The National Handicrafts and Handlooms Museum (Crafts Museum), and
The Handicrafts and Handlooms Exports Corpn. of India Ltd. (HHEC)
for the loan of pictures and permission to use them;
The National Museum, New Delhi, for permission to reproduce the image of
the Phophnar Buddha;
Jasleen Dhamija and Ranesh Ray for permission to quote from panels for an
Exhibition on Kamaladevi Chattopadhyay;
Shanta Shelke for permission to quote from her poem.

Photo credits:
The National Handicrafts and Handlooms Museum (Crafts Museum),
  pp 8, 11 to 15, 21, 28, 37, 42, 43, 44, 47, 48, 49, 54, 55, 62, 68, 70, 76,
  79, 86, 87, 88, 90, 92, 95
The Handicrafts and Handlooms Exports Corpn. of India Ltd. (HHEC)
  pp 18, 22, 23, 30, 32, 34, 36, 58, 65, 68
Avinash Pasricha pp 10, 20, 38, 45, 50, 51, 53, 56, 66, 82, 84
Anil K. Sharma/indiapicture, pp 9, 24, 39, 40, 52, 60, 72
Maryam Reshi/indiapicture, pp 25, 26, 46, 69, 74, 81
Ashok Nath/indiapicture, pp 33
B.P.S.Walia/indiapicture, pp 75
Ajay Khullar, pp 71, 77, 80
Arrt Creations, pp 16, 19

Contents

Introduction: Woven Winds 7

one
Fabric and Colour 19

two
The Magic of the Loom 31

three
Colour and Weave 41

four
Paint and Print 59

five
Embroidery, the Art of the Needle 73

six
Pallu, the End Piece 85

Select Bibliography 96

INTRODUCTION : WOVEN WINDS

Fine, so fine has this cloth been woven!
Of what is the warp made, of what the weft?
Which is the thread that has woven this cloth?

A wondrous Weaver wove this cloth,
with the thread of karma as the warp,
Memory and attachment as the weft…

Taken from two poems of Kabir, 15th century

The origins of Indian textiles are hidden in the mists of pre-history. Exactly how ancient the textile tradition is remains a matter for speculation. What is sure, however, is that by the time of the Indus Valley civilisation — about the 3rd millenium BC — cotton spinning and weaving was already an accomplishment. We know this on the basis of archaeological evidence, which uncovered

opp.
Bronze Buddha from Phophnar, 5th century AD. Even in metal, the sculptor has captured the flowing lines and sheer texture of the fabric that clothes the Divine body.

scraps of cotton cloth adhering to a silver vase. The fragments were woven and madder-dyed, showing that even at that stage there was considerable experience in the processing of colour on cloth. The discovery of terra cotta spindle whorls and bronze needles pointed to the knowledge of other fabric processes. Another find, this one from Nevasa and dated to 1000-1500 BC, was a child's necklace of copper beads strung on silk yarn and with a nep of cotton fibres, indicating clearly that silk was known and in use on the Indian sub-continent at that time. In his explorations of Central Asia, Aurel Stein found fragments of cotton and printed silk thought to be from India, at least one of which was dated to the 8th century AD.

INTRODUCTION

Chronologically the next recorded finds were at Fostat (al-Fustat) on the outskirts of the Egyptian capital, Cairo. Here archaeologists in search of ancient Roman remains uncovered a Coptic settlement near the ruins of a fort and many bits of cloth, some of which were indisputably Indian in origin and dated back to at least the 15th (some believe the 12th) century AD. The fragments are printed and resist-dyed cotton from Gujerat, and their presence on the site speaks of the medieval trade between this textile centre of western India and Cairo, poised on the east-west trade route. The fragments are distinctly of a type of cotton aimed, most likely, at a mass rather than elite market and partly comprising scraps of garments for everyday use .

But what of the periods in between these finds, the long gaps of centuries? There is little evidence in terms of actual textiles, probably because the climate in India veers from hot to cold and moist to dry and its light can be harsh and bright: not an ideal situation for preserving fabric. But much can be inferred from all kinds of sources — the great Hindu scriptures, epical literature, sculpture, the cave paintings of Ajanta, miniature and folio paintings,

opp.
Tie-dyed odhni (veil) with embroidery.

A wall hanging in kalamkari (literally, "pen work"). Such hangings could also be used as temple back cloths.

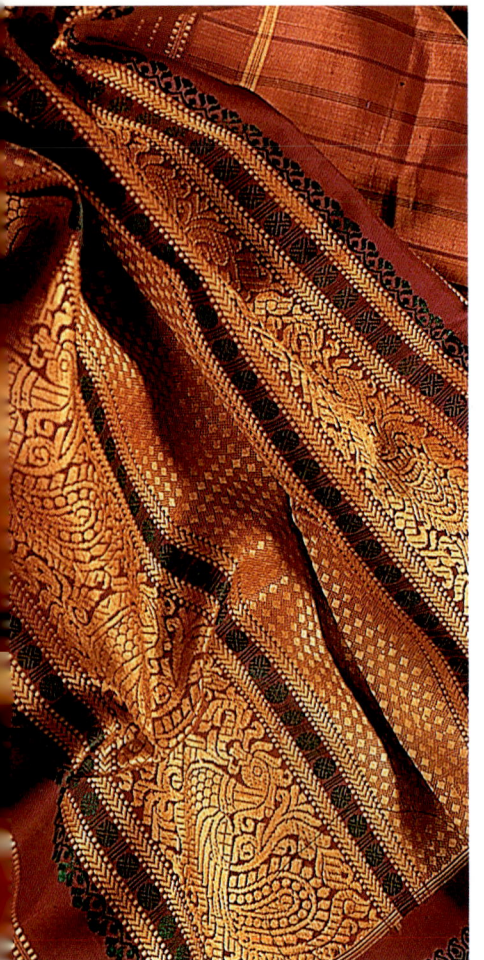

illuminated manuscripts, the accounts of travellers and historians. All testify to a glorious tradition that has remained in a full, continuous and astonishing flowering for about fifty centuries, changing and reshaping its expressions according to the creative energies of the craftsmen and the demands of monarchs and markets, evolving and innovating, absorbing and adapting the outside influences that resulted from invasions, trade and cultural contacts. Upto the 18th century no other country in the world produced such an abundance and variety of textiles; at that time India was the largest exporter of textiles.

Such are the bare facts, but they give us no idea of the range of textiles and uses to which they were put. Nor of the romance of the fabrics and the many labour-intensive, highly skilled processes that caused them to be valued so dearly.

Through the centuries, the beauty of Indian textiles drew the most lyrical and poetic expressions from those who desired them. Two thousand years ago the Tamil poets of the Sangam age compared them to the ethereal elusiveness of smoke and vapour. The Romans prized the sheer muslins of the Gangetic plains and called them "venti nebula", clouded winds, echoing their ephemeral, almost wistfully airy textures. Much later in the medieval period the poet

INTRODUCTION

Amir Khusro was to write of the same muslins: "A hundred yard of it can pass the eye of a needle, so fine is its texture, and yet the point of a needle can pierce through it with difficulty. It is so transparent and light that it looks as if one is in no dress at all but has only smeared the body with pure water." Indeed, it is said that Zeb-un-nissa, the daughter of the Mughal Emperor Aurangzeb, was once chastised by her father for appearing without clothes until she pointed out that she had on no less than eight jamas or robes!

The words used for muslins were almost lovesick in their yearning descriptions: "shabnam", or morning dew, cloth such as was transparent when moistened and stretched over blades of grass in the dawn; "abrawan", running water, fabric so fine as to be invisible to the eye when held in the flow of the stream; "bafthawa", woven winds, the lightest and airiest of all textures, floating forever in the poetic conceit of their own delicacy.

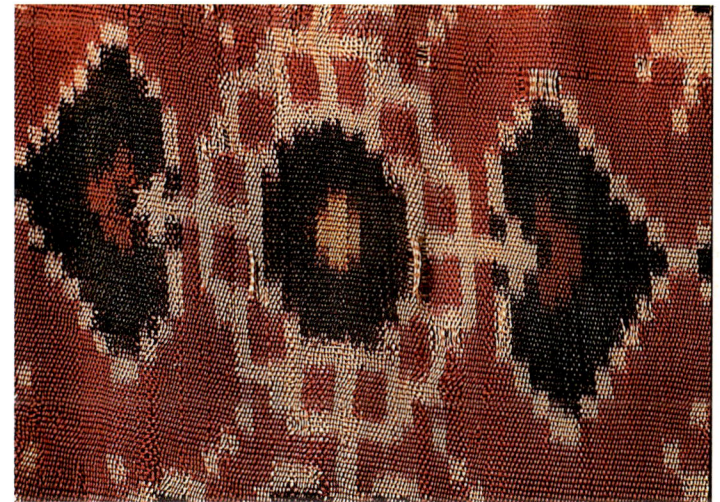

opp.
A sari from Kanchipuram, a major silk centre of south India.

Detail from an antique patola or double ikat sari. The motif, pan bhat, is in the shape of a pipal leaf.

The muslins fetched fabulous prices wherever they were sold: Rome, Babylon, Phoenicia; also in ancient Egypt, where they were used to wrap the bodies of the embalmed and scented mummies. In India, the sheerest muslin clothed the Buddha when He attained Nirvana. And when Alexander the Great came to India and triumphantly accepted the tribute of the Malavas, cotton fabric was one of the main offerings.

Muslins, however, formed only a part of the spectrum of Indian textiles. Traditionally, the processing and manufacture of textiles

Printed and painted textiles were a large export commodity.

INTRODUCTION

was the second largest occupation after agriculture; quite often the two were intertwined. Across the great swathes of textile areas in the country, from the banks of the Ganges in the north to Kanya Kumari in the south, from Gujerat in the west to Bengal in the east, thousands of families spun and wove, dyed, painted, embroidered. The range encompassed the finest of cottons and silks for kings and their courts and for the affluent, as also a variety of work cloths, cheaper and coarser textures for everyday use. Cloth was used for an astonishing variety of purposes: for garments, for painted wall hangings and travelling tents, as bed spreads and canopies, cushions and floor covers, and for headgear and robes. Embroidered and beaded, it was tenderly placed around the necks of transport animals or used as a canopy to create vivid embellishments for rural carts drawn by camels or bullocks. Woven without flaw and brocaded in gold, its perfection was a temple offering to the gods. Made to the demands of users in other countries, it formed a staple of trade, India's ancient hard-currency earner, paid for in precious bullion. So much so that at the beginning of the Christian era the luxury goods of the east, the spices, the fine cloths, the jewels, caused such a drain of gold that the wealthy Roman empire ran into a trade deficit.

A border being woven on the loom. Flowers and birds have always been favourite motifs.

Ikat from Orissa; finely-woven calligraphy, close up of a temple offering.

opp.
Pallu of a Baluchari sari from West Bengal; note the finely detailed figure work around the central motifs.

Four ships come every year from Gujerat to Malacca...
The merchandise they bring is cloth of thirty kinds, which are of value in these parts.

Tome Pires, early 16th century

They manufacture many kinds of stuffs, extremely fine and delicate, coloured for their own use, and white for trade to all parts; they call them saravetis and they are excellent for women's headgear and much valued for that purpose: the Arabs and Persians make caps of this stuff in such great quantities that every year they fill several ships with them for different places.

Duarte Barbosa, on Bengal, 16th century

East and west the textiles travelled; by land and by sea; in the dhows of Arab traders to the Red Sea and Africa or else to the Mediterranean en route to Europe; in merchant vessels laden at eastern or southern ports bound for south Asia and the spice islands. The ships carried printed cloth, striped cotton, silk fabric, fine furnishing materials. Patolas, the famous double ikats, went to Indonesia, where they were treasured as court wear and invested with sacred and ritual significance. They decorated the Hindu temples of Bali; their rags and threads were essential ingredients in

INTRODUCTION

the magical remedies of the island. Bengal alone was the centre of a huge number of export stuffs, silks and cottons, calicoes, linens, muslins, woollen fabrics. Great emporia-ports thrived on west and east coasts, prospering on the produce of their hinterlands. In the 18th century the European craze for garments and furnishings of chintz or painted and printed calicoes from India reached a hectic climax before protectionism set in and they were banned, leading to an entire — and flourishing — industry of imitations in countries such as England, France and Germany.

Another event of far-reaching consequence occurred in the 18th century. It was the Battle of Plassey in 1757; the victorious Clive annexed the textile-rich area of

Bengal as the merchants of the East India Company gradually took over the governing of India. By the 19th century virtually the whole of India was a British colony and subject to British rule. The classic principles of colonialism became reality, that colonies supply the raw materials to be turned by the colonial powers into manufactured goods, which are then sold back to the marketplaces of the colonies. In this process the manufactories of the colonised are discouraged if not shut down.

Had they sanctioned the free importation of Indian cotton and silk goods into England, the English cotton and silk manufactories must...soon come to a standstill. India had not only the advantage of cheaper labour and raw material but also the experience, the skill...of centuries.

Friedrich List, The National System of Political Economy, 1844

It was partly the flow of wealth from Indian textiles that funded the Industrial Revolution in England. An ironic situation: because that same Revolution created the textile-related machinery that was to break the back of a centuries-old tradition. Even so, as late as the early 19th century Indian textiles imported into Britain remained cheaper than local manufacture until a wall of prohibitive duties was

An old lithograph of a weaver at his loom.

INTRODUCTION

flung up. India was reduced to a supplier of cotton and indigo and forced to accept the mill-made finished goods dumped on her markets. The discovery of chemical dyes in the 19th century only exacerbated the situation. Thousands of weavers, printers and dyers, not to mention farmers of indigo, were thrown into unemployment.

It was Mahatma Gandhi who unerringly picked on the spinning wheel as a concrete example for the nationalist movement of the 20th century. Here was a tangible symbol from the grassroots that represented a means to livelihood and food for millions of people; here too a potent weapon for opposition to British power. Along with the symbol went one word : Swadeshi, of the country, echoing concepts of self-sufficiency and restoration of national pride. Indian freedom fighters threw their mill-mades from England into giant bonfires and wore handspun textiles to defy the Raj, calling them the "livery of our freedom". Gandhiji made the spinning wheel a symbol of self-reliance, investing it with the dignity of a national emblem. In so doing, he gave new life to the handloom industry of India.

Mahatma Gandhi at work on his spinning wheel.

one

Fabric and Colour

Ancient Sanskrit texts speak of four kinds of textiles from different fibres: flax, jute and hemp from bark fibres; cotton from seed fibres; silk from cocoon fibres and wool from animal hair fibres. Without doubt cotton and silk were the pre-eminent fabrics of the subcontinent, surpassing even the fine woollens for which areas like Kashmir were renowned.

The Mughal Emperor Akbar once asked his courtiers which was the most beautiful flower. Some said the rose, from whose petals was distilled the precious attar; others, the lotus, glory of every Indian village. But Birbal said, "The cotton boll." There was scornful laughter, and Akbar asked for

opp.
Clothes as communication: Rajasthani women wear turmeric coloured odhnis with tie-dyed red dots in the centre, indicating that they are mothers of sons.

Fabric was coloured red from alizarin, found in the roots of the madder plants. Alum combined to bring out shades of red and yield brilliance of colour.

an explanation. Birbal said, *"Your Majesty, from the cotton boll comes the fine fabric prized by merchants across the seas that has made your empire famous throughout the world. The perfume of your fame far exceeds the scent of roses or jasmine. That is why I say the cotton boll is the most beautiful flower."*

It is believed that the first — and, for many years, exclusive — use of cotton, the natural fibre found around the seed of the cotton plant, was confined to India during the period of the Indus Valley civilisation, around the 3rd millenium BC.

Called *karpasa* in Sanskrit, this shrub that flourished on heat and moisture was to be the prime material of the Indian artisan. In fact, wrote Pupul Jayakar, "It was in cotton that the genius of the Indian weaver, printer and embroiderer was to find its richest and boldest expression."

Harvested cotton was left in the sun for a few days to make it easier to separate the floss from the seed. It was then ginned and cleaned and carded before being hand spun into yarn. Some baked clay tools, spindles among them, have been found at Lothal, another Indus Valley site, testifying to the antiquity of the tradition. Indian agriculturists and craftsmen thus have literally thousands of years of experience in cultivating, handling and processing of the cotton plant.

Drawing out filament from the silk cocoon. Silk fabric was called "kauseya" in Sanskrit; and silken robes gifted by kings in ancient times.

> *Scarlet and purple*
> *The silkworms rise and spread*
> *Throughout Tirumal's grove...*
>
> The poetess Andal, 9th century

It is a little more difficult to date silk, *kauseya* in Sanskrit. Sericulture was a Chinese art centred around the mulberry worm, and a closely-guarded secret; an old name for silk was "chinansukh" after the country of its origin. However, silk was also native to eastern India and came from three indigenous sources, the so-called "wild silks" of tussar, eri and muga. The finest of the wild silks is the textured golden muga from Assam. An earlier muga — of which there is no trace today — was called Champa after the leaves on which the worm fed; a pure white colour, it was reserved for the kings of Assam and their nobility.

Then at some point the secret of mulberry silk was brought to India; romantic legends say it was through Buddhist monks who smuggled the eggs of the worm and the mulberry seeds in hollow bamboo canes. Other versions say that the knowledge of mulberry silk travelled from China via the valley of the Brahmaputra, or yet again on the fabled Silk Route through Central Asia and Persia. Whatever the path, it was adapted in India and soon became the preserve of royalty and aristocracy. Kings gifted silken robes on auspicious occasions and ladies of high caste wore white silk. Long loose silk pieces fluttered and floated about the body; they were called "dukula" and could be bleached or dazzling white (shveta), or dark (shyama), or even suvarna, red or warm gold.

Silk was also deemed a "pure" fabric, appropriate for religious, ritual and ceremonial occasions. Silk garments were worn at weddings and festivals and every important moment of personal and family life. Finely-woven silk was offered to temple deities; quite possibly this association with purity and ritual use led to the proliferation of silk weaving aound temple towns like Benaras and Kanchipuram. Not surprisingly, the weavers of silk were a prosperous lot. In Mandasore, in Central India, stone inscriptions mention a guild of silk-weavers who were wealthy enough to build a temple dedicated to the sun.

> *It can, however, only be a good thing to know how these peoples set about applying colours to their cotton cloths, which not only do not run or fade when washed but emerge more beautiful than before.*
>
> Journal Economique, Paris, 1752, anonymous article

There are many ways to embellish cloth; one of the most basic is to colour it.

Colour has always had a very special significance in Indian life, being invested with all kinds of social, sacred or ritual meanings. The fabric, colour and design of a garment can tell the initiated all about

opp.
Gorgeously patterned woven silk. An old name for silk was chinansukh, after China, the country of its origin.

Dyed silk yarn being carried to the weaver.

Preparing silk yarn in Vishnupur, West Bengal.

opp.
The bold and basic colours of the Indian palette: red, black, yellow. Blue, brilliant or deep, was brought in with indigo.

the wearer, who he or she is and their status both personal and hierarchical. Colours indicate seasons, emotions and states of being; they drench the tonal phrases of a musical raga; auspicious occasions are enriched by their use. They mark phases in daily life — the Mughal Emperor Humayun wore colours only according to the guiding planet of the day which dictated his activities. On Sundays, for example, he wore yellow and dealt with affairs of state, whereas Mondays were reserved for green and merry making.

The vocabulary of colour is extensive. There are three kinds of red for the three types of love, of which the deepest, most saturated madder celebrates the constancy of married love; yellow symbolises spring and its freshness, the awakening of youth and life, the colour of the mustard flower in full bloom. Indigo is for the dark pregnant clouds of the monsoon and for the Blue God, Krishna; the ochre-red of the ascetic signifies renunciation; deep rose is for the languor of a mango-scented summer afternoon. White, the colour of laughter, has many nuances: blinding white-gold, or ivorine tooth white; the softer, mistier tones of sandal white or the spent pallor of autumn cloud white.

So enraptured are we by this colour palette, brilliant and subtle at one and the same time, that we overlook the sheer skill inherent in the dyeing process. Dyeing has been known and practised in India for at least five thousand years, always as much science as art. Nothing else can explain the precision with which colour tones were achieved with the most basic of tools, those tools enhanced by profound knowledge of material and centuries of experience. The dyes came from nature, from the roots and barks of trees, from fruits, flowers and leaves, from lichens and shrubs. They strengthened the cloths they were applied to, which emerged from each wash ever more rich and glowing.

The secret of the dyes was the mordant or "fixing" agent, the magic substance that had affinity with both the cloth and dye stuff such that it could fix colour on the fabric. The mordant not only enabled colour permeation but also, used in different types and quantities, yielded tonal variations or indeed completely different colours. The mordants were, in the main, metallic salts and oxides of alum, iron and tin. Over 300 dye-yielding plants in India combined with various types, densities

Dyeing yarn in Kashmir. Dyeing has been known and practised in India for at least five thousand years.

and qualities of mordants for an incredibly shaded palette which included both dazzling primary colours and the softest of tonal nuances.

The indigo shrub and madder plants were the dyer's mainstay from the earliest times. The indigo shrub contained the blue dye agent indican, but to process the dye demanded precision. First what was called "indigo white" had to be made from the soaked leaves and an alkaline solution. Yarn or fabric was immersed in this, and the blue colour appeared when "indigo white" oxidized on contact with the atmosphere. Repeated dippings deepened the blue to a rich midnight. Red, on the other hand, came from the colouring agent alizarin, to be found in the dried roots of the madder plants and the al and chay plants. Combined with alum, this yielded shades from pale rose to dark red. But first the yarn or cloth had to be treated with oil and astringent to prevent the mordant, alum, from crystallising. Alum was the most easily available mordant and thus the most used; it was said to bring out the brilliance of colours and also render them fast.

> *Take six parts of myrobalans, two parts*
> *Of fibrous pomegranates and three parts*
> *Of turmeric and pound them all together...*
>
> From a Sanskrit recipe for hair dye, 14th century

Indigo yielded blues from deepest to palest, madder and lac the reds; pomegranate rind was added for dark green, and iron shavings with vinegar for black. Turmeric gave yellows, and combined with indigo for rich greens. Yellows came also from the safflower and the flowers of the myrobalan. Moreover, a single dye-stuff could be used with other materials for a variety of colours. The palas flower, for example, yielded a brilliant yellow. Combined with alum, it gave a bright orange; or with iron, a brownish-olive. With the coming of Islamic influences, as Pupul Jayakar has pointed out, the palette became softer, more delicate in tone, including the subtle shading of old rose, pistachio, lilac, mango-gold.

Centuries of experience had given the dyers deep knowledge of colour chemistry. But intuition and sensitivity added other dimensions and gave the artist-dyers insights into the nature and temperament of colours. They perceived subtleties of perspectives in

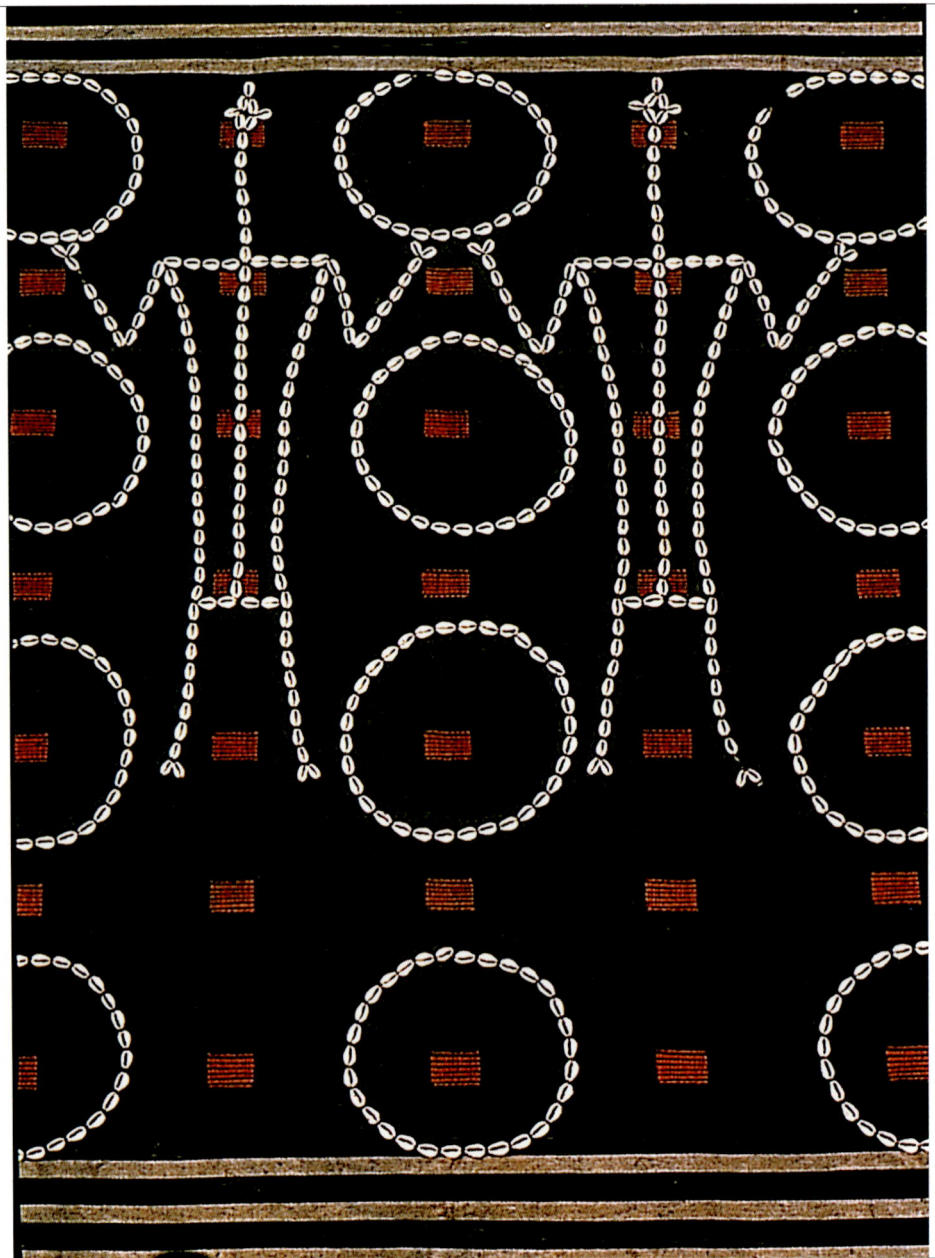

colour ranges, and could produce effects of ever-changing colour patterns in different lights. Then again, they had profound respect for their materials, many of which were believed to have healing or medicinal properties. Myrobalan not only strengthened the fabric, it also protected the dyer's body. Turmeric was a known antiseptic and madder roots were used for treating rashes and abrasions.

But the dyeing processes were elaborate, time-consuming and labour-intensive. They depended on the natural light of the sun to coax out tones, and repeated soakings in water or dye to fasten the colour. With the discovery of chemical colours things became much easier and faster. Chemical dyes could be used on all kinds of yarn and fabric. They were cheaper and easier to handle and could be transported efficiently. There was no dependence on vast supplies of water, or on plants for providing raw materials, no elaborate labour-intensive processes. Only a few pockets held out successfully against chemical dyes because of local demands or an abundance of dye plants; but in the main there was a wholesale turning to the new bright colours and consequently a loss of inherited skills.

opp.
Fabric, colour and design reveal much about the wearer. This early 20th century Naga shawl from north eastern India belongs to a chieftain's family and is adorned with cowrie shells.

t w o

The Magic of the Loom

I am the weaver, O Lord, of Thy Name;
I weave and reap the gains
Of inner harmony with Thee.
I am the weaver of the Lord's Name.

Kabir, 15th century

Imagine that the loom is set on a ring. Like all rings, it has no beginning and no end, only an eternally circular flow where start and finish melt into each other and are indistinguishable.

There is a parallel with the techniques of textile patterning. Some start on the loom, from where plain stuffs are sent out for printing,

opp.
Dressing a warp for a sari in south India through street warping.

painting or embroidering. Some fulfil themselves on the loom, where the weaver's magic is wrought to completion. And for some the cycle draws to a close on the loom as threads pre-coloured to a design are knit together into intricate motifs that were conceived and ordained before the warp was dressed.

Worked by hand by men and by women, the loom is one of the oldest and most enduring symbols of our civilisation. Because it is so old, we tend to forget that it is also a kind of machine, albeit one that relies very heavily on the skill of the human hand. There is a special relationship between the weaver, his loom and the woven cloth; and perhaps it is rooted in the ancient perception of the very universe as a fabric upon which life unfolds like a painting. The sage Markandeya is said to be the weaver to the gods whose first offering was wrought

THE LOOM

from the fibres of the lotus; it is from him that the weavers of Kanchipuram in south India claim descent.

From east to west and north to south, different kinds of looms serve different weaving needs: the simple loin or backstrap loom that literally supports the weaver; the fly shuttle loom with its frame; the pit loom where the weaver sits with his legs in a pit. Between these and other types of looms are woven the vast and astounding array of traditional Indian fabrics, from the sheerest tissues to the coarsest cloths, from silk stiff with gold patterning to the loosest of weaves, from cloths made for court and temple and trade to those made for the everyday use of common folk.

But "everyday" is not to be confused with "plain". No matter what the social circumstance, there is no poverty here of aesthetic. The fabrics, woven, painted, dyed, embellished, are an assertion of identity, as if both life's harmony and its meaning are wrenched from their threads. The simplest of clothes have a feel for the drape across the body, for the interplay of textures, for the joy of colour and the way it connects with elements of design: it is as if the fabric is permeated by beauty carelessly, almost unknowingly. It is an

opp.
Pallu of a sari. The play of black and white and the gold edging add elegance and sophistication.

Loin loom, Arunachal Pradesh, in north east India. This simple backstrap loom literally supports the weaver and is widely used throughout the north east of the country.

33

An ikat sari of Orissa on the loom.

unselfconsciousness born of centuries of practice and knowledge of material. Such ease belies the complex series of stages required to prepare the yarn for the loom and to finish the fabric afterwards.

The yarn must be bleached, dyed if need be, wound onto bobbins and warped. The common warp methods today are street warping, where stout posts and sticks are used to hold the yarn in place; or drum warping where the warp length is drawn on to a drum. The weaving process is as simple or complicated as the fabric demands. The warp yarn is stretched on the loom, awaiting the shuttle that will fly from side to side with the weft, which will be carefully tamped into place. This is the basic, baldly stated. But there will be many variations. Is this a jamdani? Then two weavers will patiently sit at the loom, with their patterns on paper placed under the warp, with cut threads precisely positioned ready to be locked into place with bamboo sticks and a sley so that the pattern slowly forms as the extra weft is worked in. Other weaves will place their own demands.

Volumes could be filled to describe the different types of textiles and the techniques that go into their making. To attempt description now is a challenge of selection, at best an arbitrary categorisation or a dictionary approach. Should we think in terms of textile use — court, temple, trade and folk— in the classic manner of a museum? Or simply in terms of plain and patterned? By fabric, or by process? A dilemma indeed. Whatever the consideration, there will be omissions, but a beginning has to be made somewhere.

For purposes of convenience, we shall look at fabrics thus — firstly, dyed and woven; secondly, painted or printed or both; and thirdly, embroidered. These are arbitrary divisions that cut across the organic and sophisticated nature of textiles in India. Because certain processes encompass more than one aspect, there could be overlaps and cross references. Take, for example, printing, which itself allows for many variants.

Firstly, there is the direct application of colour and pattern to the surface of the fabric. This is done by using a wooden block (block printing) or a silk screen (screen printing). An embossed variation can be achieved by a process called roghan, which is described later in the book.

Then there is what is known as the indigo or resist process, in which portions of the cloth are covered with a "resist" substance, which could be wax, clay, gum or resin. When the cloth is dyed, the parts covered with the resist do not take the colour — they "resist" it. Why was it called the indigo process? — because indigo was a colour that was applied

directly to the cloth and did not need a mordant; therefore, when dyers applied indigo, all portions that were not to be blue were covered with the resist material. Resist is put on with a brush or a block or by hand and removed after the dyeing.

But there is also the critical role played by mordants in dyeing. The process called mordant, madder or alizarin (the last two names presumably because it was largely used for red, of which madder and alizarin are sources) uses the magic of colour chemistry to give the cloth glowing hues. As we have seen, mordants are not only "fixing" agents for dyes, but also bring out tonal variations within a colour when applied in differing intensities. For example, alum used as mordant with madder could produce shades from pale pink to deep red. And when different types of mordants are used the resultant reactions between dye and mordant can produce completely different colours. In this process, mordants are applied with brush or block to the cloth as required by the pattern that is to be created. The cloth is then dyed; the chemical reaction will produce the desired colours, but only on those parts of the fabric that have been treated.

These processes are not necessarily mutually exclusive. Chintz, for example, was stencilled, mordant-dyed, resist-dyed and painted on cotton. That is to say, the design was transferred to the cloth, the reds and black dyed through a mordant, the blues with indigo and the other colours — yellow and green —were

WOVEN WONDER

pg 36
Silk warp on a horizontal warping drum before it is rolled on to a warping beam.

pg 37
Baluchar sari, silk brocade on silk. The elaborate pallu has floral cones surrounded by figures of men on horseback.

A classic combination of black and gold in this brocaded silk sari.

painted on, green being brought about by the blue/yellow combination. We may imagine how many times a single piece of cloth had to be treated, printed or painted, dyed and washed, then multiply that by the number of pieces made for sale or use!

Printing is about working on woven cloth; however, the patterning of fabric can begin even before it comes on to the loom, at the stage when the yarn is dyed. In the most famous example, that of double ikat —which we shall see later —the yarn is dyed in such a manner that warp and weft mesh in the weaving to create beautiful motifs. Exquisite motifs are also part of the magic weaves such as jamdani and paithani or the brocades of Benaras, all of which were executed by highly skilled craftsmen, true artists of the loom whose work was worn and treasured by generations of Indian women. In the post-loom stage the fabric can be embroidered, or printed as detailed above. It can also be decorated and made colourful through the process known as tie-dye, a resist-dye technique that depends on parts of the fabric being tied or shut off from the dye.

It was in the combinations of these processes that Indian textile genius lay. Each new permutation was like a new creation filled with a lively spontaneity. Variations were not a cause for alarm; they were the craftsman's breath, giving freshness and vitality to the fabric, spurring him to greater flights of the imagination.

Children watch an ikat sari being woven on the loom in Orissa. Most of the Orissa looms are pit looms.

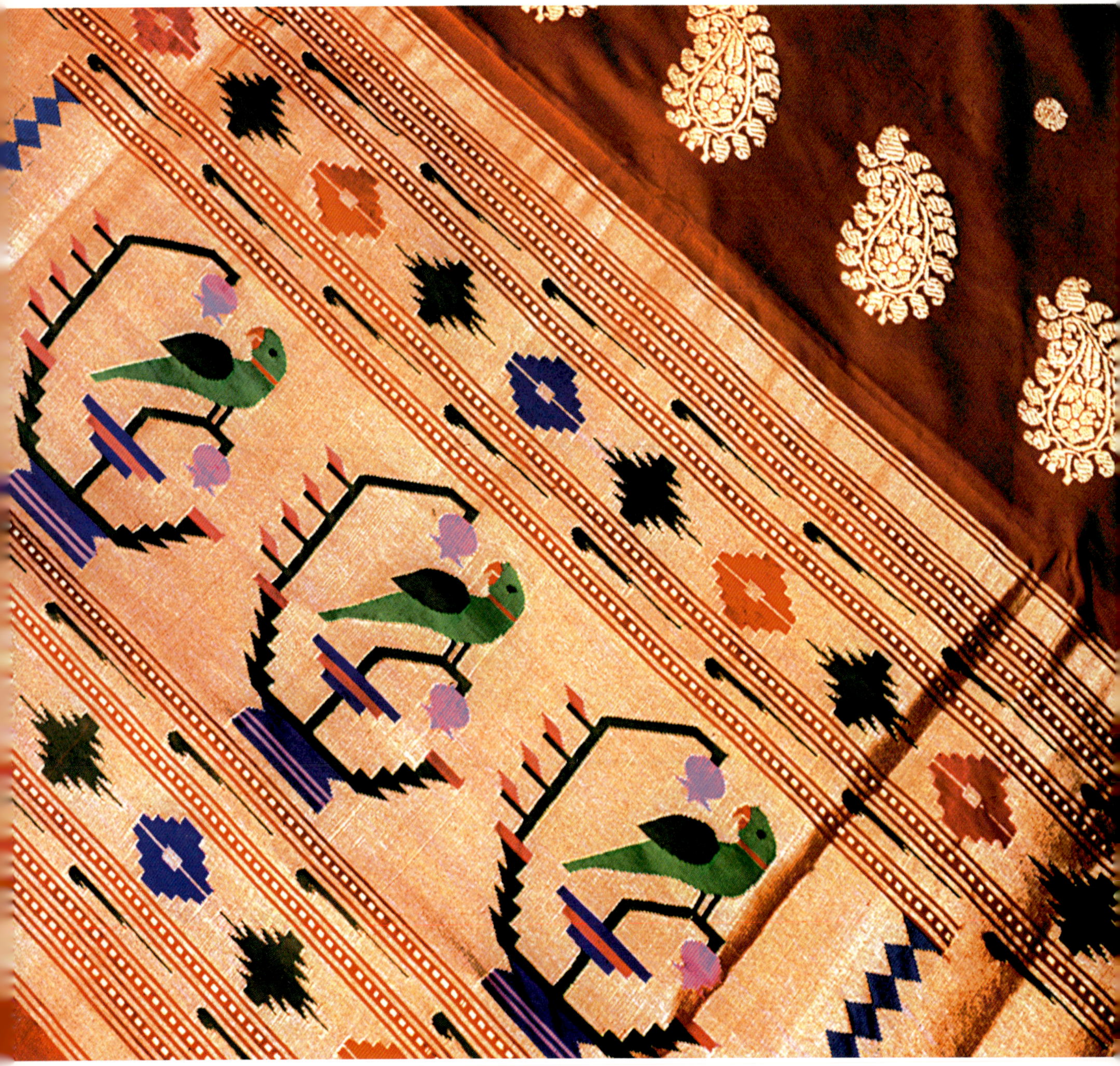

three

Colour and Weave

The loom is a magic place, a metaphor used by poets all over the world to express many concepts. It is where life's warp and weft come together to form a fabric; its shuttles move back and forth to click out the passage of time; its frames are draped with dreams woven and unwoven.

In India, the loom is the sari, measured to the amplitude of this timeless dress which leaves the loom ready to be worn. If we look at the sari, however, what is it except a length of cloth of five and a half metres? The sari is defined by its wearer, the woman whose person

opp.
A poem in silk and gold: pallu of a Paithan sari from Maharashtra.

it adorns: it takes her shape, is pleated to mould her body, its endpiece, the pallu, floats over her shoulder or is brought across the front. In former times, the choice of sari and its method of being worn indicated clearly her social status and where she came from, the pattern and colours often dictated by tradition and occasion.

The sari has travelled a long road. In classical sculpture and in painting we see its ancestor, a shorter version, a lower garment knotted at the navel and girdled at the waist which was called by many different names, including "antariya" and "vastram". The girdle had small bells attached to it which could signal the seductive approach of a beautiful maiden; as she walked, the flow of the drape was revealed "as moonlight on the tulip or dew drops on the morning rose". These words of Amir Khusro were written in a completely different context but are equally and poetically apt here. The intrepid traveller Ibn Batuta describes an unsewn garment secured at one end and used to cover breast and head at the other; though there was also a veil like an odhni which was often decorated. When there was an upper garment, it was a breastband tied at the back (uttariya), or a simply stitched blouse.

Gradually the sari took its own shape and regional variations. Some pleated it at the back; some wore it in a nine yard length pleated and drawn between the legs to be tucked in at the back. Colour, fabric and motif were drawn from local traditions and influences. The names of weaving towns became synonyms for their saris, names like Chanderi whose fine textures, gold borders and pastel colours were an essential part of a woman's wardrobe, Benaras for brocade, Kanchipuram for its intricate silk-and-gold weaves, Baluchar for its elaborate pallu with figures and horses and elephants, Paithan for its jewel-like colours and the richness of its weaves. Some saris depended entirely on weaving to bring out their beauty; in others, dyeing played a major part in design and pattern.

Resist-dyeing or tie-dye gave rise to two famous traditions, those of bandhani and ikat. There are many variations of tie-dye, since some processes use tie-dyed yarn, where the pattern emerges in the weave of the fabric. Elsewhere, tie-dye refers to the process undergone by the fabric itself, the term for this being "bandhani" as it is called in Gujerat and Rajasthan, the two main areas where the technique finds expression. Here the fabric is knotted tightly with thread in a pattern and dyed repeatedly to produce the design. The tied parts do not take the colour and so the design is produced.

Bandhani is a process that demands time and patience. In the first stage, the pattern has to be transferred to the cloth. The cloth is

opp.
A "butadar" sari in coarse cotton from Orissa, with motifs of fish and flowers sprinkled across the body and border.

At the loom in Sambalpur, Orissa, a major ikat centre.

WOVEN WONDER

folded over, and then one of several methods is used: Either the dampened cloth is pressed over a block which has the pattern in nails or pins. The pressure "raises" the cloth, which then is pinched up and tied. This is not much in use today. Another method is to stamp the pattern with a wooden block and yet another is to have plastic with pin holes arranged in the design which is then given a removable colour wash so that the imprint remains, much like a stencil. Dots, squares, circles are the main elements of design, and they form the many patterns we see on bandhani, the elephants and flowers and figures.

Once the pattern is on the cloth, the material is painstakingly pushed up, pinched and tied with thread. In Rajasthan, the nail of the left hand little finger is grown long for this purpose, but in Gujerat it is the finger which is used. The areas to be left undyed are tied first as the fabric takes the lightest colour of the dyes to be used. It is

opp.
Tie-dye odhni, c. early 20th century. The satin veil cloth is joined in the centre and filled with foliage in fine dots.

Swathes of brightly coloured tie-dyed fabric, some of which are still knotted to show that they are genuine.

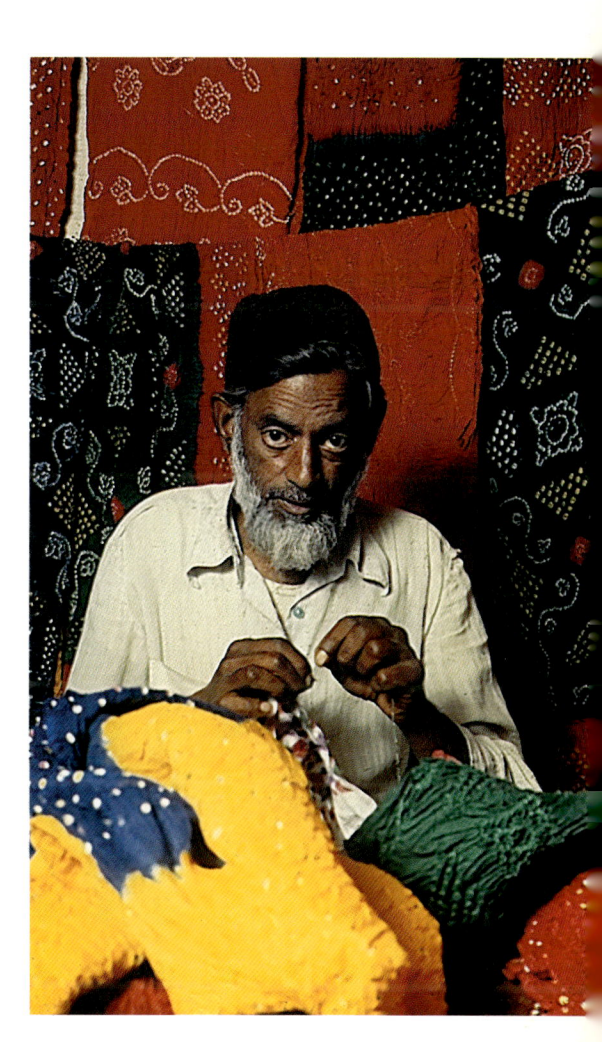

opp.
The famous double ikat, a stunning traditional patola from Patan.

Strips of diagonally rolled fabric unfurl to show the characteristic "wavy" pattern of leheriya.

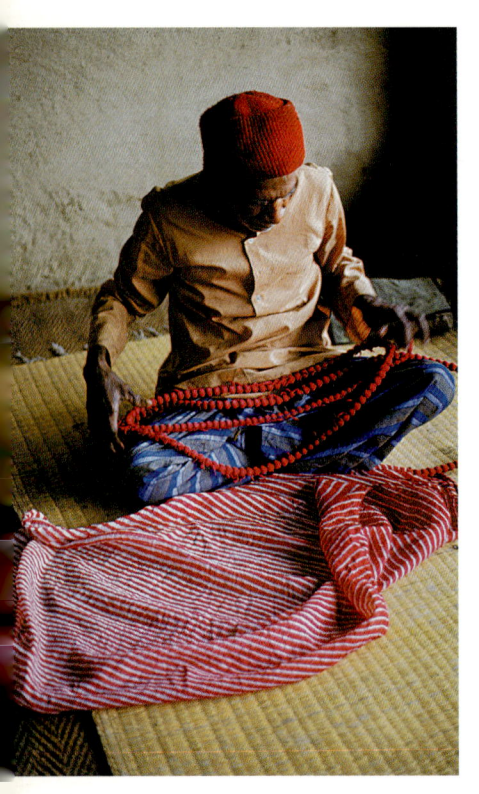

then dried. Further tying takes place of those areas meant to retain the lightest colour and then the next dye is applied — and so it goes, tying and untying and retying, until the darkest colour has been applied. It is work of minute and meticulous application, and if there are a large number of colours this can indeed be a lengthy process! An intricate sari could have as many as 75,000 dots. The dyes can be applied by hand rather than a bath, by smearing a piece of dye-soaked cloth over the required areas. The edges are wrapped in paper or rags to prevent them taking undesired colours. Obviously, the colours and their order of application are carefully worked out before the process starts.

A bandhani garment was considered auspicious for a bride, so it is little wonder that there are special designs for the occasion, such as the "chandokhni" and "shikhara". The "barah bagh" opened out to reveal the twelvefold flower garden, and there was even a "bavan bagh" or fifty two: this is now rare because of the labour involved. The most famous of the wedding saris is the gharcholu, divided into squares with bands of gold with elaborate patterns in each square. The number of squares is ritually significant and has to be in multiples of nine, twelve or fifty two.

The principle of tie-dye also applies in leheriya, literally "waves", so called after the wavy pattern the process produces. Here, fabric lengths are rolled diagonally from corner to selvedge and tied tightly at intervals, then dyed so that the unbound parts take on the colour. The fabric has to be thin so that the colour can penetrate its rolls. The result is a series of diagonal stripes. Again, the fabric can be tied and retied to produce more than one colour, or rolled in the opposite direction to get an interesting multicoloured chequered pattern.

The sari is brightly coloured with these methods, but so are turbans and odhnis and dress lengths. Often, both bandhani and leheriya fabrics are sold with the tied knots still intact to prove that these are indeed tie-dyed and not printed.

Speak of resist-dyed yarn for weaving and you are immediately in the area of ikat, a fabric of such great mystique that till today it remains amongst the most expensive and valued of all Indian textiles. Indeed, it has always been so: on the islands of Indonesia it could be worn only by royalty and Indian ikat was a thriving export item. The word itself is derived from the Malay "mengikat", meaning to tie or to bind; and this tying or wrapping is the secret of ikat. Bundles of yarn are wrapped according to a pre-determined pattern, and when dyed, only the open parts take the colour. Colours can be added by rewrapping the yarn, always being careful to follow the pattern, which is generally worked out on graph paper. The warp must be meticulously positioned for the loom to work its magic, and when the yarns are woven, complex designs in brilliant colours emerge on the finished fabric.

Usually it is either the warp or the weft yarns which are tie-dyed.

There are three well-known groups of ikats, of which the most prized is the silk patola from Patan in Gujerat, the famous double ikat, where both warp and weft yarns are separately wrapped and dyed with such precision that they line up on the loom and mesh to form the most intricate floral and geometric patterns. The result is one of great richness and depth, where both sides of the patola look alike. This incomparable heritage is said to have entered Gujerat in the 12th century when weavers from Maharashtra and Karnataka came to work under the patronage of the Patan rulers, the Solanki Rajputs. As many as seven hundred are said to have migrated; today there is only one family left, the Salvis of Patan. They weave their magic on the simple-looking loom using natural vegetable colours, of

The golden gleam of brocade is vivid in this close up of a border.

pg 48
An unusual pallu of an unusual sari. This made-to-order Orissa ikat is woven from an Indonesian design.

pg 49
A rare patola, c. mid-19th century. The unusual striped turmeric ground is complemented by typical patola borders and pallu.

opp.
Pallu of a sari, timeless dress that leaves the loom ready to be worn.

which it is said that they are so fast that they will not fade even when the fabric is old and worn.

The pipal leaf (pan bhat) is a recurring motif. Jewel-like reds and greens and deep blues are the most favoured ground colours for figures of birds and animals and flowers. The weaving of such fabric is not just complicated, it is also time-consuming, a single sari taking upto seven months and the labour of two men to complete. No wonder, then, that the patola symbolises the greatest of wealth and refinement and is often worn at weddings, each festive piece carefully preserved to hand down as a family heirloom.

Orissa is another major ikat centre, where the form is locally known as "bandha". There is, however, much difference between this and the patolas; here, the designs seem to flow more in curves and this may be because the tying is very fine, done on thin yarns and with only two or three threads as compared to about twelve in Patan. Another feature of these ikats is that some areas of the pallu and border are woven rather than worked in ikat, the weave being carried out often with an extra weft. The Meher weavers of Sambalpur say that this strengthens the fabric. Apart from Sambalpur, the main ikat areas include Sonepur and Bargarh.

Nature is undoubtedly an inspiration for the themes of bandha, and takes stylised, almost fantastical forms. Floral designs include eight and ten petalled flowers, called "aath phulia" and "dus phulia" respectively. Creepers and lotuses are generously used, as are elephant and swan motifs along with stylised fish, birds, the auspicious conch shell and rudraksh beads. Bold geometrical patterns in reds, whites and blacks catch the eye, either circles or bright coloured squares of varying sizes.

The third major ikat area is Andhra Pradesh where the start of the tradition is an interesting story. The fabric was called "telia rumal", literally, oily kerchief, so named because it was originally a multi-purpose square which could be used as a lungi, a shoulder cloth or turban. Oil was profusely used in preparing the yarn for weaving, which added to the name. The tradition was on the verge of dying out when it was rescued in the mid-fifties and its techniques extended to the weaving of saris and fabric lengths. Pochampalli, Chirala and Puttapaka are the main centres today. The original colours that distinguished the telia rumals were various shades of red and deep blue with small geometric designs. Traditional patterns borrowed from Patan and

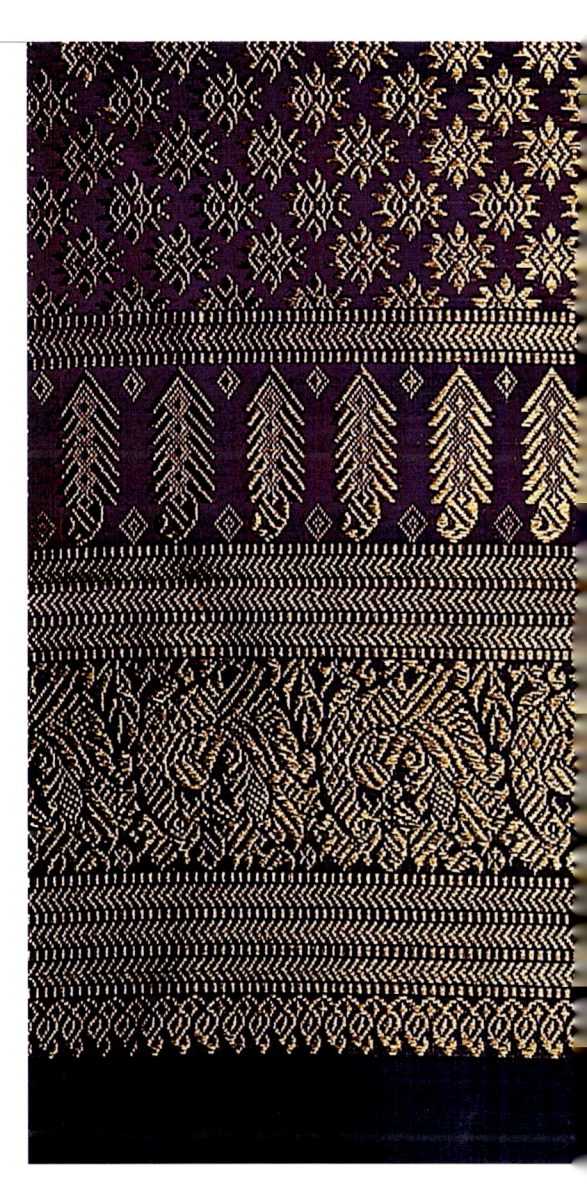

Orissa and modern designs in abstract motifs and bright colours are also very popular here.

Quite another kind of magic is wrought on the loom with brocade. Brocade, too, has a long history in India, spread across centres like Paithan, Benaras, Murshidabad, Surat and Tanjore. The richness of the brocade sari made at least one such mandatory in a bridal trousseau and there was ample choice.

Paithan, located on the northern bank of the Godavari river, is one of the oldest cities of the Deccan; it is Pratishthan of the Satavahanas. Here from ancient times was practised the art of tapestry weave, a method of creating patterns with the weaving-in of multiple weft threads in different colours. It is said that this technique was brought into India from central Asia and was adapted by the skilled weavers of the Deccan. A poem in silk and gold, they called this brocade; it was known to the Greeks who traded the gorgeous fabric for gold and jewels. Today, centuries later, the Paithan sari remains amongst the most cherished of traditional fabrics, its sumptuous texture enlivened by woven borders and the lavish pallu. Woven in pure silk with gold borders, a single sari can take between two months and two years to make; such is the painstaking workmanship that at times only a half inch of the sari is woven in one day. The ground colours are brilliant, deeply shaded with reds, pinks, the characteristic purple, blue; on this appear the stylised motifs, the

COLOUR AND WEAVE

opp.
Delicate gold brocading being done on the pallu of a Kanchipuram sari in south India.

Magnificent Benaras brocade, gold and silver flowers on a rich red ground. The combination of gold and silver is known as "Ganga-Jamuna".

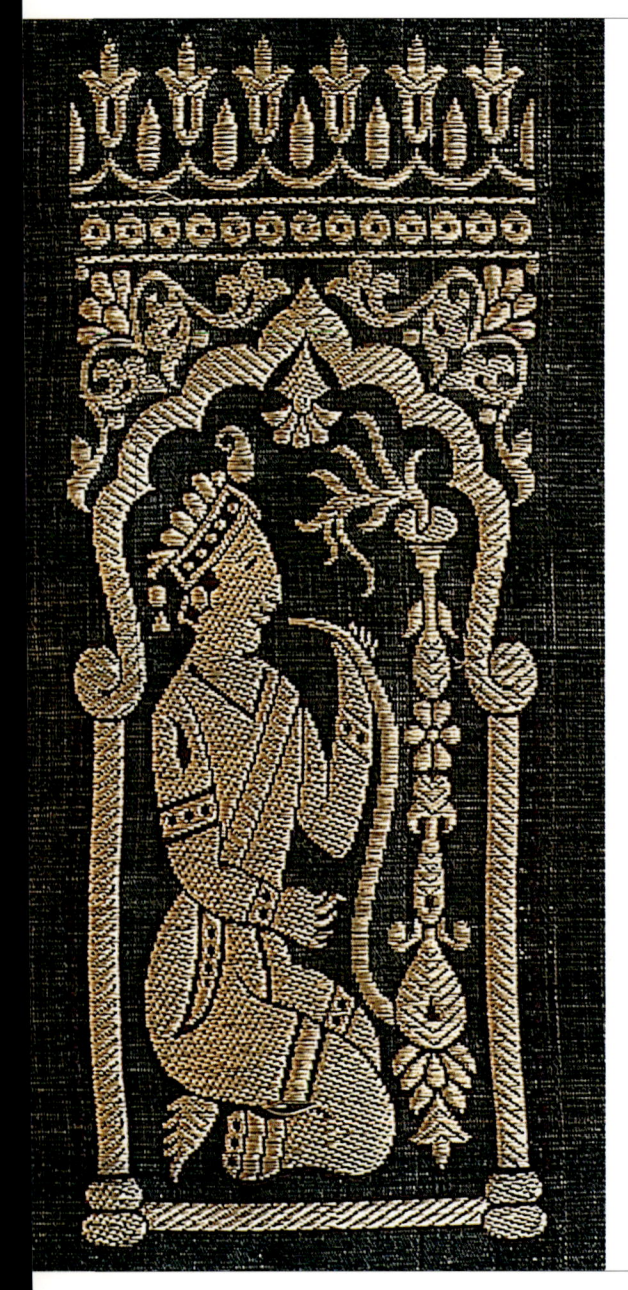

parrots, peacocks, floral vines, the mangos and coconuts. Saris are named after the principal motifs, such as "tota-maina" (parrot) or "kairi" (Mango).

But say "brocade" and most people immediately think of Benaras, whose silk brocades are world famous. They have been given the romantic name of "kimkhab", the "little dream" in Persian; another interpretation gives this the meaning "woven flower" from the Arabic. Looking at the rich beauty of this work, one could say that either meaning is accurate. A Benaras silk sari is traditionally in a single colour with motifs and patterns woven in gold or silver threads. This intricate technique calls for the services of a naqshband or design master who is adept at creating patterns or "naqsha pattas" drawn on graph paper, and making samples of these with threads tied onto the loom so that the weaver can follow the design. As the weaving takes place minute shuttles of gold thread are worked through the warp to form the many motifs; once the motif is completed, the gold thread is knotted and cut. The more delicate the motif, the more complex the task of weaving it.

COLOUR AND WEAVE

The ingenuity and colour palette of the Benaras craftsman remains endless. Geometric and floral designs predominate, particularly the "buti" or flower, of which alone there is a huge variety; then too there are the running patterns of leaves and flowers known as "bel" which again have many variations. Zari, the gold or silver thread used for the patterning, is the soul of the brocade. In earlier times, the zari would be made of gold or silver wire drawn out so fine that it could be woven; now, of course, the cost would be prohibitive and gilted threads are used instead. Ground colours range from shades of red and crimson to old rose; blues from the palest sky blue to turquoise and lapis lazuli; saffron and buff and bright orange. Deep colours, like purple and black, made certain designs stand out dramatically.

Well to the east of Benaras is the home of yet another renowned brocade tradition —that of the Baluchari, which takes its name from a village in Murshidabad district of Bengal. Murshidabad was a thriving trade centre for silks from the 17th to the 19th centuries, but the weaving of the brocade got its greatest impetus from a Nawab who not only patronised it but also decreed that its elaborate style be used only by nobility and royalty! Perhaps this is one reason for the traditional Baluchari themes that are lavished on the pallu; they seem almost narrative, as if telling stories of the court, since

opp.
Man smoking hookah: a motif woven on a Baluchari sari.

pg 56
An elaborate figurative design worked in silk brocade.

Brocaded cotton: the famous jamdani or figured muslin from Bengal.

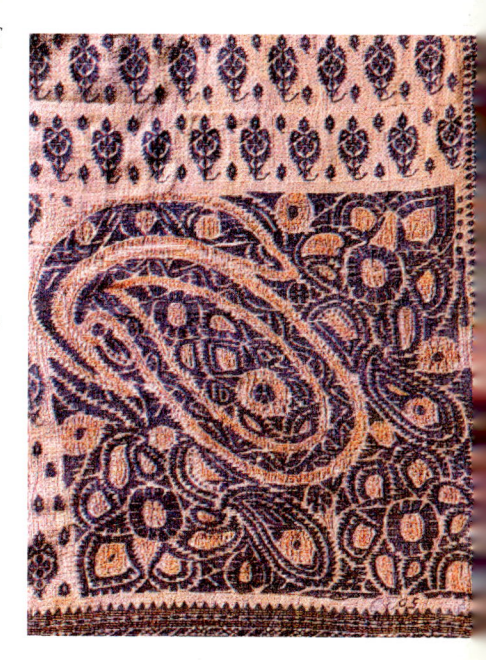

they are figured with kings on elephants, men on horseback or smoking hookahs, graceful dancing girls. The ground colours are deep, such as maroon, purple and blue. Small butis cover the field and florals decorate the borders. At its zenith, Baluchari weaving used only pure mulberry silk threads and no gold or silver zari. Some decades ago, the production of this brocaded silk had almost come to an end, but it was revived in Vishnupur in Bengal.

A thicker silk forms the ground in Kanchipuram, Tamil Nadu; here, the silk thread used is actually three threads twisted together, one reason why the fabric is heavier and stronger than many other types of silk. Rich colours, often with contrasting borders and pallus, are woven with zari in motifs such as the rudraksha, or the perennial peacock and parrot. Most of the raw silk comes from neighbouring Karnataka; and in contrast to the antiquity of many other textile traditions, that of Kanchipuram silk weaving is just a couple of centuries old.

Another speciality of Tamil Nadu is the temple sari woven as an offering for deities in a temple. Heavy with gold and with broad borders, the temple sari must be flawless to be worthy of being offered to the deity.

Of the brocades in cotton, the most famous is the jamdani or figured muslin whose original home is Dhaka in present-day Bangladesh with other important centres in West Bengal and Uttar Pradesh. Jamdanis may recall to us the description of a costume by a classical Sanskrit poet who speaks of a garment white as foam, of the finest muslin, embellished with flowers and birds. On fine cream or white muslin jamdani weavers worked ornate patterns in coloured cotton yarns and sometimes in gold, the yarns for the patterns being usually heavier than that used in the ground. The most sophisticated were those which were patterned white on white, the one appearing almost as a tonal variation of the other. The designs were worked in by hand as extra wefts by two weavers sitting side by side using individual spools of cut thread called "tillis". Such painstaking workmanship resulted in elegant motifs, such as the chameli or jasmine and the leaf patterning.

These are only a part of the riches of the Indian loom, fabrics, textures and designs perfected for sale to kings and merchants and for export. The patronage of princes and emperors led to the creation of karkhanas or workshops where skills were encouraged and experience developed. Each region had its own special textiles and weaves. In addition there were the coarser weaves for everyday use; these too had their own language of colours and motifs.

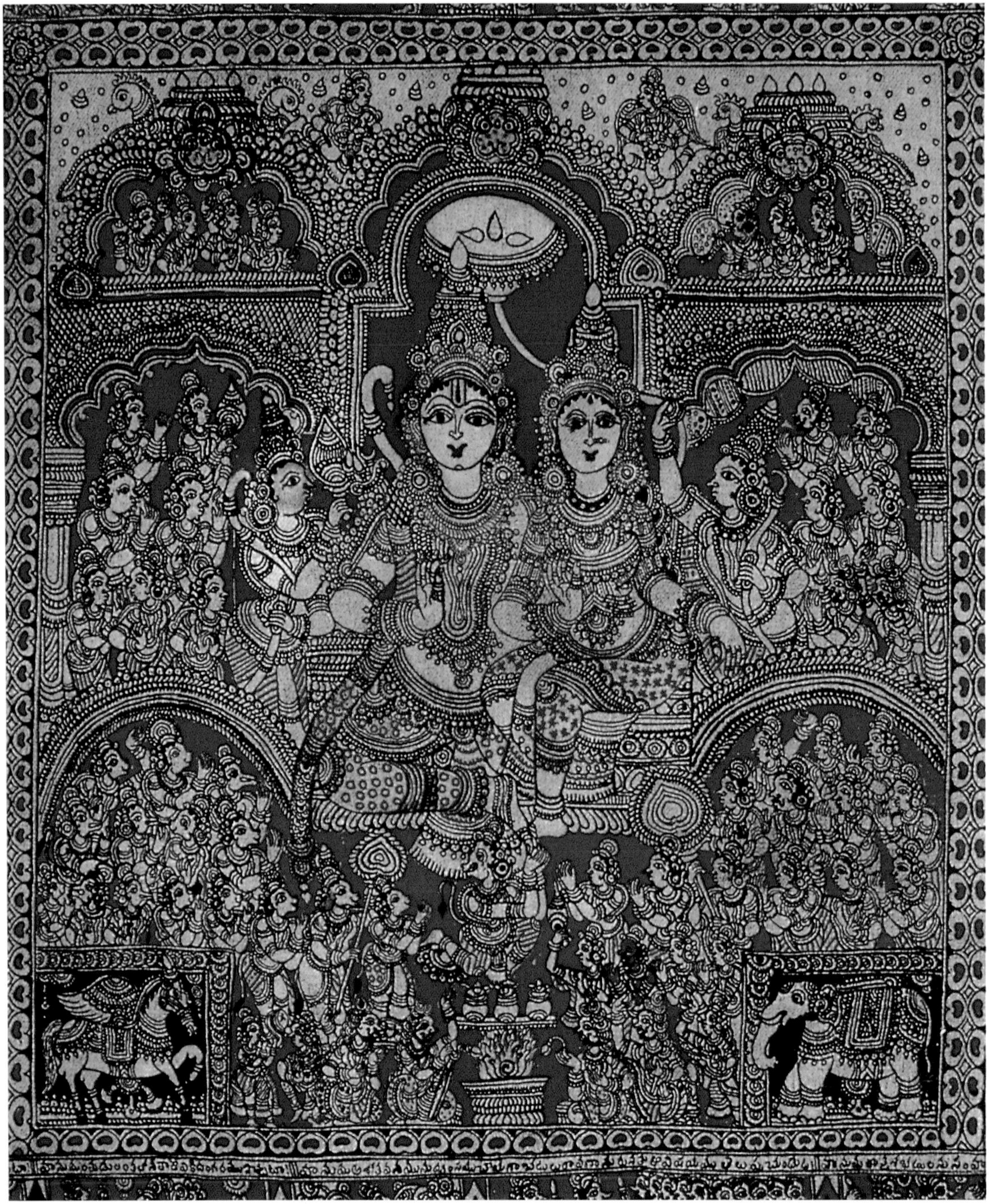

four

Paint and Print

There is a strong tradition in India of painted and printed fabrics which were used for a variety of purposes. Some were religious, painted cloths meant for temple backdrops, like the pichhwais of Rajasthan consecrated by the Vallabhacharya sect to Lord Krishna as Shrinathji. The Lord here is Shyam, the Dark; his elongated eyes look upon Radha, the gopis and the cows with benign and compassionate love. There are, too, the shrine cloths of Gujerat called Mata-no-Pachedi, votive offerings to the Goddess when misfortune was averted, block printed and dyed and showing her divine image enthroned or astride an animal. Some cloths were made for trade, like the cottons of Masulipatnam which were

opp.
Kalamkari wall hanging from Srikalahasti depicting Rama and Sita in epic narrative style.

A kalamkari artist at work. In the style of Srikalahasti, hand painting continues to dominate, the themes being from the great epics.

exported in large numbers to different destinations and designed accordingly. Some were meant for narrative purposes, rather like giant illustrations carried from one place to another by itinerant story tellers. In this category come the brilliant red scrolls of the Pabuji-ka-phad of Rajasthan, where the heroic deeds of the legendary Pabuji are sung to this day by Bhopa minstrels. Or the vigorous figures of the patua painters of Bengal who unscrolled their paintings as they recited their tales, each frame related to a part of the narrative.

This too was the origin of kalamkari of modern-day Andhra Pradesh. Stories from the great Hindu epics were painted on cloth, the textile equivalent of temple murals, and local bards used these to illustrate their recited verses. The master craftsman of kalamkari, Shri Guruppa Chetty, is quoted as saying that the art is mentioned in the two thousand year old Amarkosha as "flags decorated with writing in cloth" and that it flourished under the Vijayanagar kings and Golconda Nawabs. Kalamkaris were also temple back cloths. But the traditions of the major kalamkari areas developed in different directions, which also led to differing techniques.

The word "kalamkari" means pen work; the name is derived from the kalam or pen with which the designs are traced. Kalam itself is a Persian word, and its use originated from the trade between Persia and the Deccan Muslim kingdom of Golconda. In the 17th century Masulipatnam (Machilipatnam) became a renowned centre for the manufacture and export of painting on cotton using vegetable colours. This was also known as chintz, but at some later stage the nomenclature got confused by all patterned cloth, whether painted or printed, being called by this name.

Masulipatnam designed primarily for the Persian market, and its prayer mats and hangings were embellished with the delicate florals and tree motifs so beloved of its clientele. Srikalahasti, on the other hand, specialised in temple or religious cloths for its Hindu patrons, kings and merchants alike, figurative hangings depicting epic legends and gods and goddesses. But then new tastes and new markets emerged; of necessity, the design vocabulary had to change, enlarge, to encompass the needs of clients. When the

Europeans became buyers, they put the fabrics to varied uses: as garments, as bed covers (palampores), chair covers and curtains. Florals predominated as did a kind of Chinoiserie much in vogue at that time. When trade with the west declined, so did the output.

Towards the middle of the 20th century kalamkari was relegated to near-obscurity and barely a handful of artists were left. It is thanks to the efforts of Kamaladevi Chattopadhyay and the All India Handicrafts Board that it was revived in the mid

This antique kalamkari, c. 18th century, depicts an entire Vaishnavite pantheon, which includes the Dashavatar as also scenes from Krishna's life and the glories of Vishnu.

'fifties and given a new lease of life. Textile scholar Jasleen Dhamija recalls travelling to Srikalahasti with Kamaladevi in 1956, at a time when no one had heard of kalamkari, to meet master craftsman Jonnalagadda Lakshmaiah. He was persuaded to train his son and other young men in the art; sitting in his room, the first Apprentice Training Scheme under Master Craftsmen was devised, through which the master would be paid an honorarium and the students a stipend. In Jasleen Dhamija's own words:

> In 1958, when the All India Handicrafts Board had a limited budget, the scheme started with a tiny amount, less than Rs.10,000 and a beginning was made to revive a dying art. Kamaladevi bought the cotton cloth and gave an advance to the master for purchasing materials to prepare the dyes. Young boys began to learn to process cloth, prepare dyes and draw the minor figures.
> The work of the first batch was displayed which created great excitement — and one batch followed another. Over the years the number of practitioners multiplied. Today there are over a thousand kalamkari artists…many of these masters work with their wives. A new dimension has been given to kalamkari which has grown into an exciting contemporary form of expression.

There were, of course, other centres famous for kalamkari, but Masulipatnam and Srikalahasti remain the principal ones, and it is interesting to look at the different techniques used in both. Masulipatnam, as we have seen, was an export area for Persia and itself under the sway of the Qutbshahi rulers of Golconda. Moreover there were present on the Coromandel coast Persian craftsmen to work or supervise the output from the area. Stylised flowering trees, such as the images of the Tree of Life, were featured rising from colourful plants with a profusion of trailing flowers and buds, long-tailed birds, perched peacocks whose fans looked bejewelled: in short, a sumptuous ode to life. Yet the whole was so delicately conceived and executed in subtle colours that it had a quality of rich restraint. Similarly, the hangings of mihrabs or arches were presented with grace, often with cypress trees in the centre. The very themes suggested that patterns would be repeated, especially as the output was created for export sale; and with that came the use of the printing block to replicate the elements of the painting. Thus the Masulipatnam kalamkari used both print block and pen, a practice that continues to the present time.

In Srikalahasti hand painting still continues to predominate, as do the figurative and the narrative work with episodes from the Puranas, Ramayana and other epics as the themes. The subjects demand a kind of spontaneity and creation anew that cannot be achieved with a block. Newer kalamkaris include Christian themes such as the Assumption of Mary and the Crucifixion of Christ, or Buddhist themes such as the life of Buddha. The style is distinctive: rounded figures with large eyes lend a pleasing grace to the narrative, which is often depicted in panels around the main figure. The Srikalahasti style is closer to its antecedents since it continues to use only the kalam: two types of kalam actually, a pointed sharp-tipped one for outlines, and a round flat one for colour infill. The kalam is equipped with a pad that holds the dye, whose flow on the fabric can be controlled by exerting more or less pressure on the pad.

PAINT AND PRINT

The Tree of Life — pictured here in close up — was one of kalamkari's most favoured themes. Such stylised trees, birds and flowers were the hallmarks of exports to Persia.

Graceful arches and slender cypress trees are replicated in this elegant and sophisticated kalamkari example.

The kalamkari process from start to finish is laborious and slow, involving resist dyeing, painting and printing. As many as seventeen different stages have to be undergone with repeated washings of the cloth, each to be done carefully and correctly for the required result.

The "kora" cotton cloth is first bleached by immersion in a solution of goat or buffalo dung, washed in water and then dried in the sun for a few days. Next, the cloth is mordanted in a myrobalan solution to which buffalo milk has been added. This prevents the colour from spreading in the next step. Then a fermented solution of rust iron and jaggery is applied, as freehand drawing with the kalam in Srikalahasti, and with wooden print blocks in Masulipatnam. This clear solution comes into contact with the myrobalan treated cloth and turns black. Now all the areas meant to be red are painted or printed over with alum as mordant. After this, the cloth is left for a at least a day before the excess mordant is removed by washing the cloth under running water. Red colour is dyed by boiling with the appropriate dye stuffs, alizarin or madder.

From this point on, the process differs between Masulipatnam and Srikalahasti. In the former, all the areas that are not to be blue are covered with wax applied with a kalam, and the waxed cloth is immersed in indigo solution. The wax is then removed by boiling the cloth in water. Yellow is painted on to produce yellow and green, and the cloth is finally washed and dried before the final colours emerge. In Srikalahasti, the cloth goes through further mordanting in alum and dyeing in reds: this is so that tonal difference between the reds is achieved, the background being deeper than the figures. The final colours are painted on with the kalam, first yellow and then blue. Once, the only colours used were the famed vegetable dyes. Today more chemical dyes are used, though now there is a strong trend to return to the old traditions and revive the colour skills of olden days.

Quite different from kalamkari but also interesting is a process known as roghan. This is a pigment of a sort applied directly to cloth. Roghan means oil or fat, and that forms the basis of this thick, bright paste. The oil of safflower, castor or linseed is kept on a slow boil for 12 hours and then poured into cold water. This produces a residue which is mixed with chalk, pigment and a binding agent.

The roghan can be applied to the cloth in two ways. One is to draw out a thin string with a rod, which is then traced over the cloth like an embossed pattern. The other is to stamp the roghan with metal-faced blocks. Either way, the fabric is folded over vertically and horizontally and pressed, so that the design is transferred to the rest of the cloth. When gold or silver powder is sprinkled over the paste, it is called "tinsel" or 'khadi", and produces a charming effect rather like raised and glittering flowers all over the fabric. There was a time when roghan was extremely popular and its use widespread on all manner of fabrics from saris and dupattas to curtains and cushion covers. Today it is still practised mainly in areas of Gujerat and Rajasthan.

Block printing is a skill that has been historically famous. Its practice calls for extreme precision, and that meticulousness begins with the making of the blocks themselves. For example, for a detailed Tree of Life, almost one hundred different blocks could be used! The block maker was no less a craftsman than the printer or skilled dyer; his work place was like an atelier where artists chiselled and carved on wood to perfect blocks with the most delicate of designs. Most designs were traditional, such as flowers, vines, mango motifs, but an artist could add to his repertoire by bringing in variations on familiar themes. The blocks were made of seasoned teak or sheeshum wood, and it was accepted that the finest came from Pethapur near Ahmedabad and Farrukhabad in Uttar Pradesh, as also Jaipur. In some areas, block making was a specialist function; in others, the printer made his own blocks.

A typical block print on cotton, handprinted yardage most commonly used for garments.

pg 68
An example of roghan from Kutch.

pg 69
A chhipai or printer carefully presses his block on the fabric.

opp.
Bagru print from Rajasthan. The colours are warm, traditionally deep reds and blacks.

Before use, the blocks were, and continue to be, soaked in oil for softening.

Once the cloth has been prepared for printing by being washed, bleached and dyed (if necessary), it is stretched and pinned over the surface where printing will take place. How complex the next steps will be depends on how many colours are to be printed on. A multi-coloured fabric takes both time and skill; not only does the operation have to be repeated, but the positioning of the block has to be precise. In direct printing, the printing is usually done from left to right and it is the outline that is applied first; then the second colour with a point on the block serving as a guide for the repeat impression, and so on. Different dyes are used for silk and cotton.

The block printing areas cover many parts of the country, Gujerat, Rajasthan and Maharashtra in the west; Madhya Pradesh and Uttar Pradesh in the centre and north; and in Andhra Pradesh and Tamil Nadu in the south. In this widespread and prolific industry, many styles have met, merged, been exchanged or adapted. Some centres remain renowned for their prints, such as the distinctive ajrakh of Kutch in Gujerat and Barmer in Rajasthan which is direct and resist printing in madder and indigo. In fact, the very word ajrakh derives from the Arabic word for blue and the fabric was traditionally in blue and red. In Rajasthan, Sanganer and Bagru are well known printing centres. The work of Sanganer, near Jaipur, is usually on white or pale grounds and patterned with cool, stylised floral sprays, cones and butis scattered over the field. Bagru's colours are warmer, deep reds and blacks.

Block printing is one of the ways of giving a fabric colour and design to make it more beautiful and vibrant. Its versatility allows it to be used for embellishing all manner of cloths: from those that we wear to those that we use, such as quilt, bed and pillow covers, wall hangings, floor coverings and yardage.

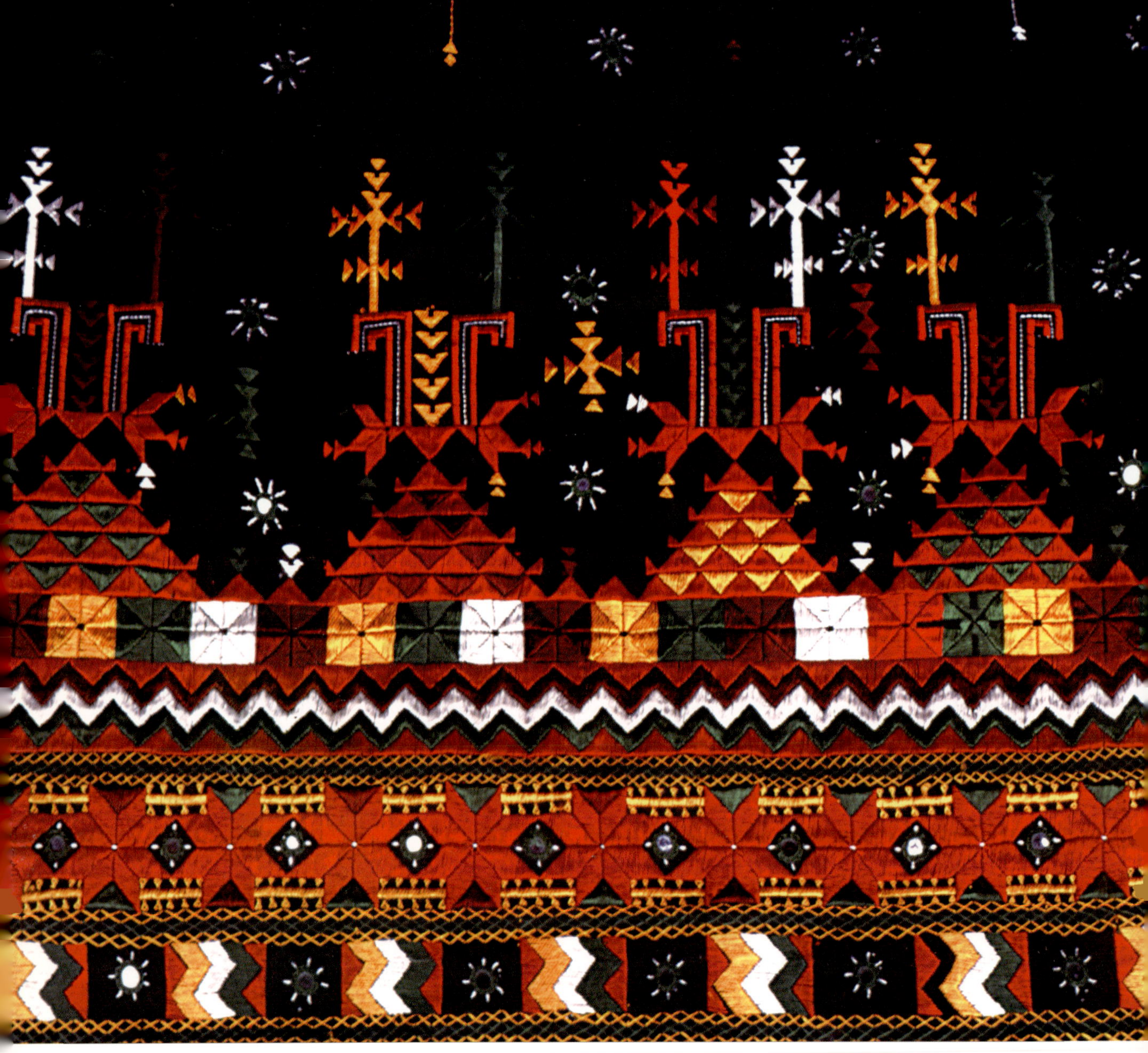

five

Embroidery, the Art of the Needle

That embroidery has been a traditional art both professionally and at home is a matter of record. Bronze needles were found at Mohenjodaro, the Indus Valley site — though it must be said that their use specifically for embroidery has not been established. Around the 4th century BC, the Greek geographer Strabo describes Indians dressed in "richly flowered muslin"; by the time of the Mughal era Indian embroidered muslin was famous throughout the world. During the reign of Emperor Aurangzeb, the French traveller, Bernier, writes of Imperial karkhanas or workshops for various crafts and arts, among them a hall of embroiderers who worked under the supervision of a master and created fabrics "enriched with

Embroidery from Gujerat. Intricate needlework and bold colours are set off by the use of mirrors.

these fine needle-embroideries". There were embroidered garments, gorgeous patkas or waist bands, wall hangings and floor coverings. Embroidered quilts were a major export item from Gujerat.

But away from this opulence there is a whole area of embroidery as home craft done mainly by women either to sell locally or for their own use. Here, another kind of richness prevails, a vibrant and energetic display of colour and design that catches the eye whether one looks at the work from Gujerat and Rajasthan or Punjab. Very often, the embroideries are what scholar Judy Frater has poignantly termed "threads of identity", revealing caste, place of origin and the epics of community—histories of a people stitched in the most eloquent language they know. The skill is transmitted from mother to daughter to grand-daughter, along with the aesthetics of colour and design.

Kutch woman in Gujerat working on embroidery.

opp.
Birds and foliage are vividly executed, as in this peacock, a favourite motif.

Without doubt, it is the Gujerat/Rajasthan belt that dominates in the sheer exuberance of its intricate embroidery. Here it is used in such profusion that it is not merely embellishment, it is a vivid manifestation of life itself, splashed across quilts and on wall hangings, on cradle cloths and decorations to cover the horns, necks and backs of animals. Garments for celebratory or ritual occasions, such as weddings and fairs and festivals, are decorated with brightly-coloured stitches in motifs of flowers, birds and animals. In earlier times, the Mochi craftsmen of Gujerat used to work embroideries professionally for sale to the affluent ladies of the local courts, or to merchant and landowning families; from them, it is said, came the famous ari-bharat work, which uses the awl to execute the stitches. But in the main it was, and is, the domestic craft of the women and girls of the house, the younger generation learning from the older. They wield their needles like paint brushes and often execute their own dowries, not just costumes and wall hangings but also the square decorated chaklas in which they are wrapped and finely worked torans to hang over doors as an auspicious symbol of welcome.

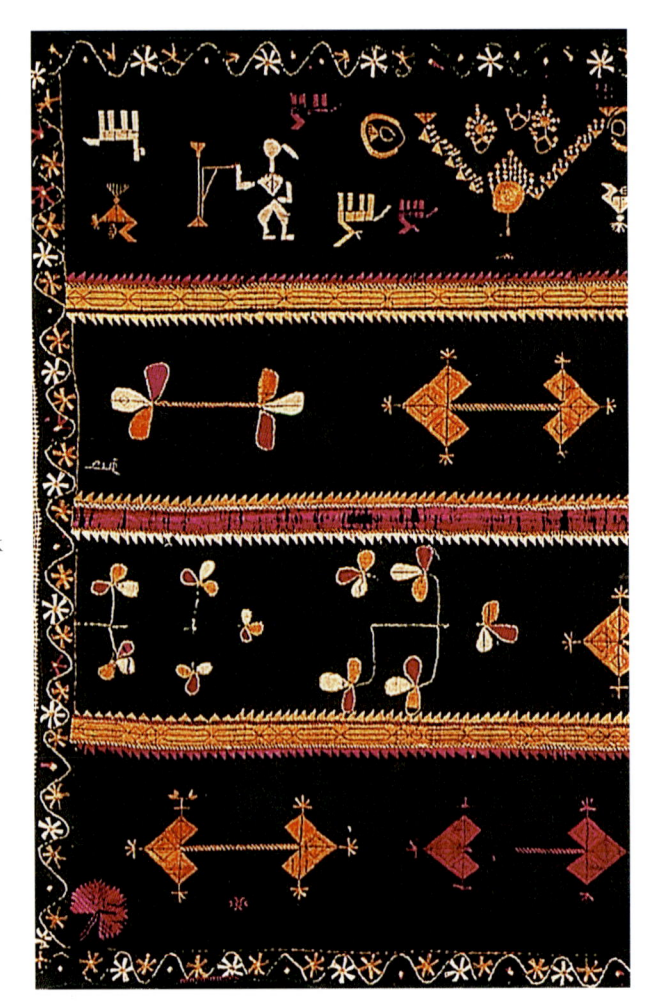

Each area, each community, has its speciality in terms of the types of stitches used, favoured motifs and even colours. Traditional Rabari embroidery is done in cotton or silk thread in bright reds, greens, yellows, oranges, using stitches like herringbone, square chain, double button hole and running stitch. But even here there are variations between the Sorathi, Rajkot and Patan Rabaris with the addition of applique, mirrors, tassels and fringes. Kathi embroideries use chain stitch or an long darn stitch called adiya fatiya, and are famous for their depictions of the romance between the Rajput Verawal and the Kathi beauty Rupande.

Above all, it is the richness of colour that attracts the eye. Lozenges, flowers and squares in deep colours—purple, scarlet and blazing orange—are embellished with mirrors that flash and gleam from the centre of the motifs. Medallions are finely detailed with geometric patterns. And although today stitches and motifs have travelled between areas, it is still possible to distinguish the chain-stitched peacocks of the Rabaris and the parakeets and flowers of the Ahirs.

Bright jewel-like colours remain a characteristic of the Punjabi phulkari as well. The word literally means "flower work" and to craft this embroidery was both a labour of love as well as a happy domestic social occasion. Originally phulkari was done for use within the family only. The women of the house

opp.
An unusual example of phulkari from the early 20th century. Naïve geometric motifs contrast with a top panel of figures.

A lady's dupatta with a chiffon base and fine ari and zardozi work in silver and gold.

would get together to stitch, though not on the same piece, and girls learnt from older women. The cloth, a deep rich indigo or madder, is a coarse local weave which is durable and allows the embroidery technique to be done easily. In phulkari, the design is embroidered in darn stitch on the reverse of the cloth over counted threads. Only one thread is taken up at the pick of the needle so that the pattern can be counted; a long stitch is left on the right side of the cloth. Thick floss silks are used for the embroidery, which can be in both vertical and horizontal darn stitches, creating an interesting shaded effect as the light plays with the gloss of the silk.

The skill of phulkari is enriched by family pride and love. When a baby is born, the grandmother rejoices with prayers and a distribution of sweets; she then sets to work on an embroidered piece called "bagh", literally, garden, which is patterned all over. The bagh acquires ceremonial significance as grandmother plies her needle over the years, embellishing the coarse, dark khaddar cloth with lozenges, flowers, sun, moon, trees and other motifs in glossy orange and gold and red. The bagh will be given to the grandchild on her wedding day, or to the bride if the grandchild is a boy. Little wonder that such cloths become family treasures to be cherished as much for the nurturing love that created them as for the fineness of the needlework. In another version called chopey, it is the maternal grandmother who makes the phulkari, this time stitching along the edges in double darn stitch which is the same on both sides of the cloth; this will be draped on the shoulders of the bride during the wedding ceremony.

opp. : Chamba rumal (kerchief) from the early 20th century has the delicacy of a miniature painting of the Pahari school; likewise, the theme is mythological, that of the abduction of Rukmini by Krishna.

EMBROIDERY

In contrast to the robustness of phulkari is the delicacy of the Chamba rumal or kerchief, originally used as a covering for gifts offered on ceremonial occasions or to temple deities. The rumals were also used as backdrops or canopies for the deities in a temple. This is the simplest of stitching on fine muslin cloth, using running stitch for outlines and darn stitch for the infill so that the effect is the same on both sides. The appearance is perhaps not as vivid as the work of Gujerat, but it is certainly elegant of line and soft of colour. Scholars have often likened the Chamba rumal to miniature paintings of the Pahari school, calling them their textile counterparts; probably because the themes derive, like the paintings, from mythology and the stories of the Bhagavat Purana. Flowers and animals are featured along with finely-drawn figures to create charming tableaux, such as the Radha-Krishna scenes with trees, water and a moon, or the Ras-Leela with Krishna and the gopis.

The famed "whitework" chikan embroidery from Lucknow.

opp.
Women working on crewel embroidery in Kashmir.

The same simple yet sophisticated charm permeates an altogether different embroidery, the kantha of Bengal. Originally the kantha was a practical means of re-cycling fabric to form soft cotton quilts, coverlets, pillow cases or wrappers; seven types of kantha have been listed, each with its own motifs. Old saris, usually in white or cream, would be stitched together in layers of four or five, the oldest and most worn at the centre, and deep red and blue threads drawn from the edges of saris would be used for the stitching and embroidery that decorated the surface. Thus fabric that would otherwise have been thrown away was re-used, all the softer for having been washed and worn for years. Running stitch supplied the outlines and darn stitch the infill; these were stitched through all the layers so that the fabric appeared the same on both sides. The work of kantha shows a fine eye for detail and begins from the centre of the piece with a lotus motif that is said to represent the universe, radiating outward to create fantasies of flowers and birds, animals and fish, whorls and spirals. Again, those who have studied kantha draw a parallel between this and the alpona or rice-flour paste decorations traditionally done in Bengali homes on auspicious occasions.

Puthukulli, the woven and embroidered shawl of the Toda tribe of south India, has a bold black and red design.

No mention of the embroiderer's art could exclude chikan, centred in Lucknow, which is worked on tanzeb, the local fine, light muslin. Called "whitework" or "white embroidery", this is one of the most skilled and painstaking of needlework forms and its appearance is one of exquisite beauty, quite in keeping with the refined aesthetics of the Nawabs of Awadh who once patronised the art. Sprays of flowers, vines, mango motifs scatter the fabric; and the delicacy of chikan entails several types of stitches being used for maximum effect along with jali, or the pulled thread work that looks like miniature lace. Bakhia, or the back stitch filled on the wrong side to create a subtle shadow, is one of chikan's best-known stitches, as is the applique-and-cut work and there is the use of tiny satin stitches to produce raised work like french knots. The detailing is very fine and delicate.

The embroidery of Kashmir probably deserves a volume by itself for sheer range and delicacy. Its application is so varied, ranging from shawls to wall hangings to rugs to garments. The craftsmen — and this is one of the areas where embroidery is a male as well as a female art — are inspired by the beauties of nature that surround them and turn to motifs such as the "ambia" (mango) and "boteh" (flowers) and the chinar leaves. Delicately shaded pastels on white or pale grounds are embroidered in a fine and detailed manner. Among the best known styles are the sozni, generally worked in panels along the sides of a shawl, using a stitch like stem stitch in an outline form. Sozni is often done so skilfully that the motif appears on both sides of the shawl thus naming it "dorukha" or with two faces.

Ari, or hook embroidery done with an awl, the famous crewel work of Kashmir, employs motifs of flower designs finely worked in concentric rings of chain stitch. A range of colours is used for this art which decorates articles such as cushion covers, bed covers and table cloths.

Far from the delicate vines and trailing flowers of the Kashmir Valley is the bold geometric design used by women of the Toda tribe who live in the Nilgiri Hills around Ootacamund (Udhamangalam). Their weaving and embroidery skills are well-known, and shown to great effect in the puthukulli, a shawl with woven bands worn like a toga during ceremonial rituals. The embroidery is done between the bands and dextrously worked by counting threads in such a striking manner that the bold red and black appears woven.

Handworked embroidery is an arduous art. Once transmitted from mother to daughter, part of a proud dowry tradition where the work travelled with the bride to her new home, social change is reshaping many expressions of this art. The old lines between commercial and domestic are blurring, so that the work that was once done in homes for the family —kantha, for example, or phulkari —not only becomes available to a wider world but also changes in its application.

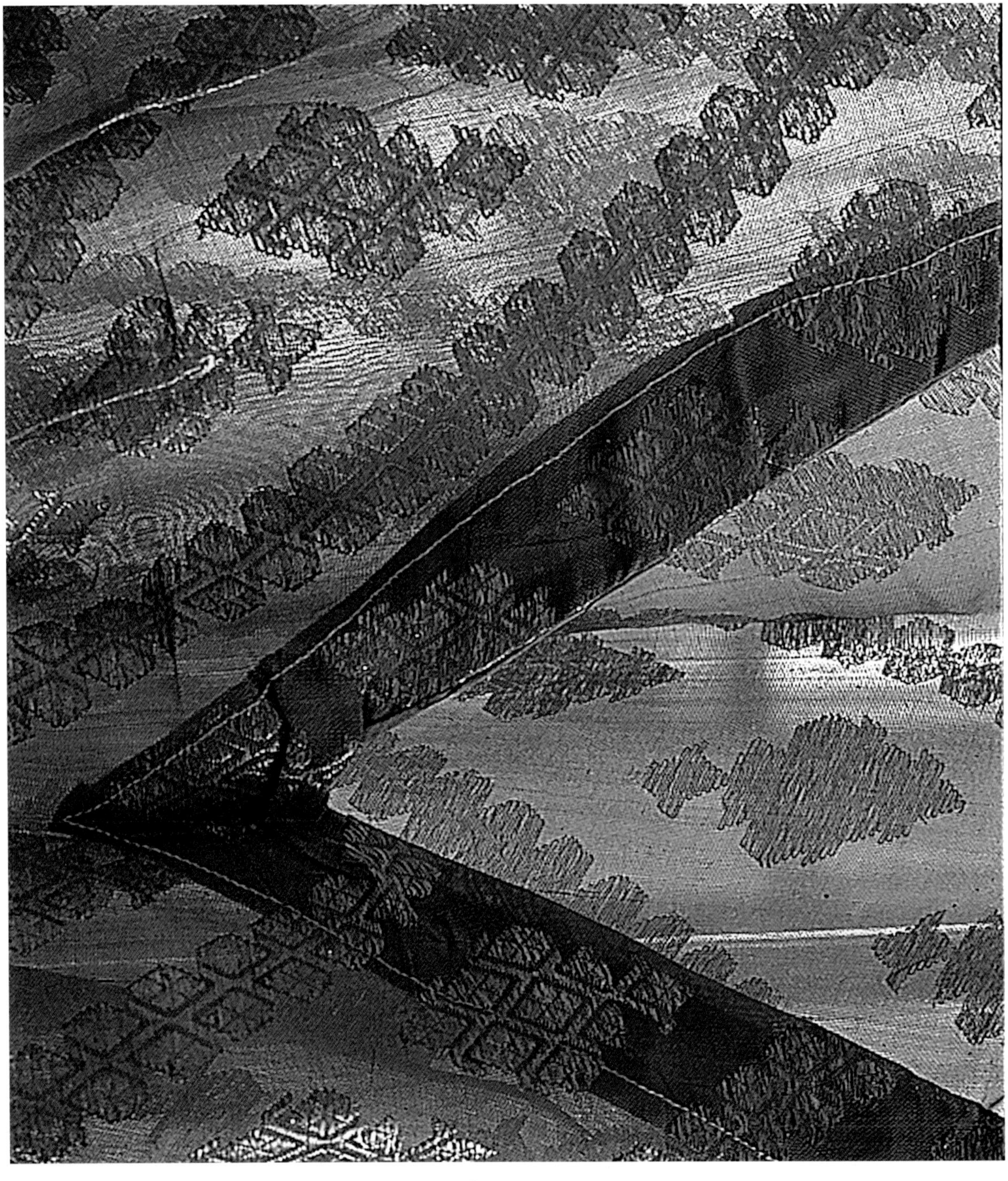

six

Pallu, the End Piece

There are moments when I hold the Paithani
Close to my heart as close can be,
Its soft, silken caress
Brings my grandmother back to me.
The intervening years vanish,
Time's broken thread runs whole again;
O golden squares of my grandmother's saree,
Tell her of my wellbeing then....

Shanta Shelke, Marathi poem

As long as there remains the handloom sari and women to wear it, there will be the weaver, the block printer, the embroiderer, the dyer...so goes a saying. Nostalgia and melancholy wrap the memory of old saris, for we know we shall not

opp.
Light, gauzy, airy of texture: the fine brocade tissues of Benaras.

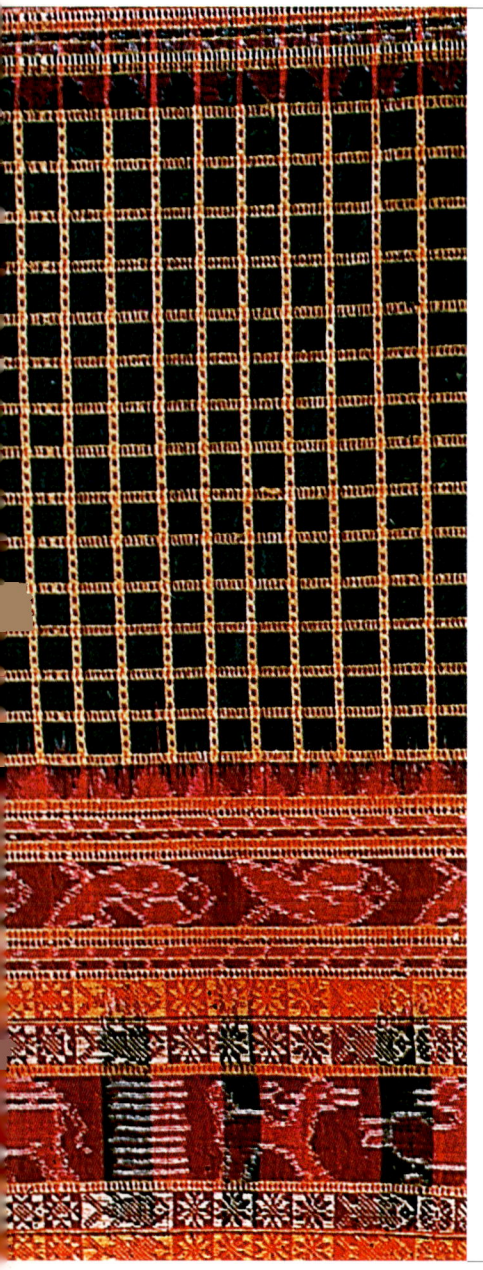

see the like of some of them. We store textiles that can no longer be worn simply to gaze at them again and again and marvel at colours and motifs, a delicacy of design, a fineness of weave. Some may never be repeated because there are no craftsmen or no buyers left, times have changed…

The rapidity of changes in styles, in fashions, in costumes have made handlooms particularly vulnerable. There was a time when all crafts, textiles included, had an assured place in our homes and lives. Unlike in the west, "crafts" were not just decorative pieces, they were a way to make our lives more beautiful by adorning everyday objects so that the purely functional was transformed into textures, shapes and colours that would be pleasing to use. Garments and cloths were purchased because of tradition—a bride would, for example, include in her trousseau certain definite and unchanging textiles from a regional repertoire—or because they were clear indicators of caste and community. Such factors are no longer as important as they used to be.

Moreover our economy has changed and so has its scale. Mass produced mill-made goods are cheaper, as many women have found out; those saris and garments are also more practical for a busy housewife, they don't need to be starched or ironed to look their

END PIECE

best. There is also the quest for "modern" from the mass market, which has turned its attention from the rough textures of handwoven to the shine of synthetics. All this has more than a faint irony to it considering that the handloom revival was born from nationalist sentiment and that handlooms remain to this day a subsidised industry.

In the heady days after Independence, the movement for revival picked up strength and brought together remarkable people and a remarkable cause. It was recognised that handlooms were not only an endangered heritage, they also gave employment and food to millions across the country and their further income potential was great. It was the Government which took the initiative by establishing the All India Handlooms Board in 1952 to coordinate production, design, marketing and technical development. Later, in 1955, the All India Handloom Fabrics Marketing Co-operative Society was set up, a body concerned with the marketing of handloom goods. The thrusts since then have included the setting up of Weavers Service Centres to provide design inputs and document and revive traditional designs; and Indian Institutes of Handloom Technology for the upgradation of skills. It is interesting to note that the Charter of the Weavers Service Centre mentions sourcing design ideas from museums, temples, palaces and books of art, as also

opp.
Sachipar cotton sari from Orissa.

A senior member of the Salvi family of Patan, the only surviving weavers of the famed patolas.

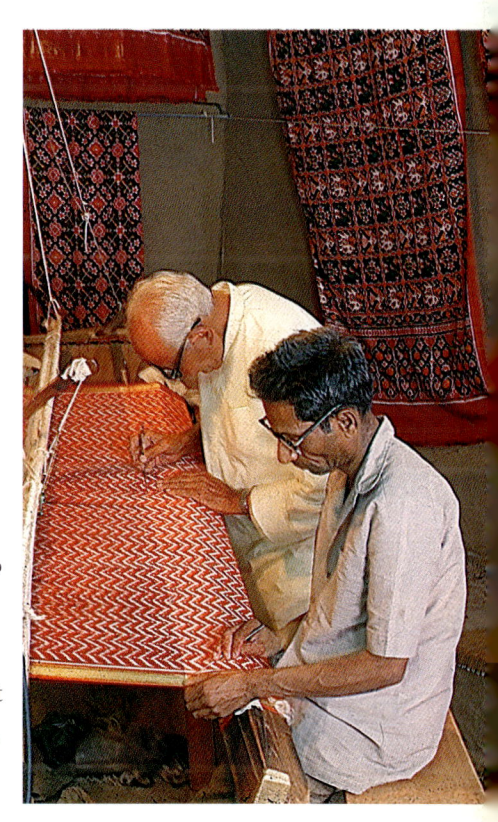

WOVEN WONDER

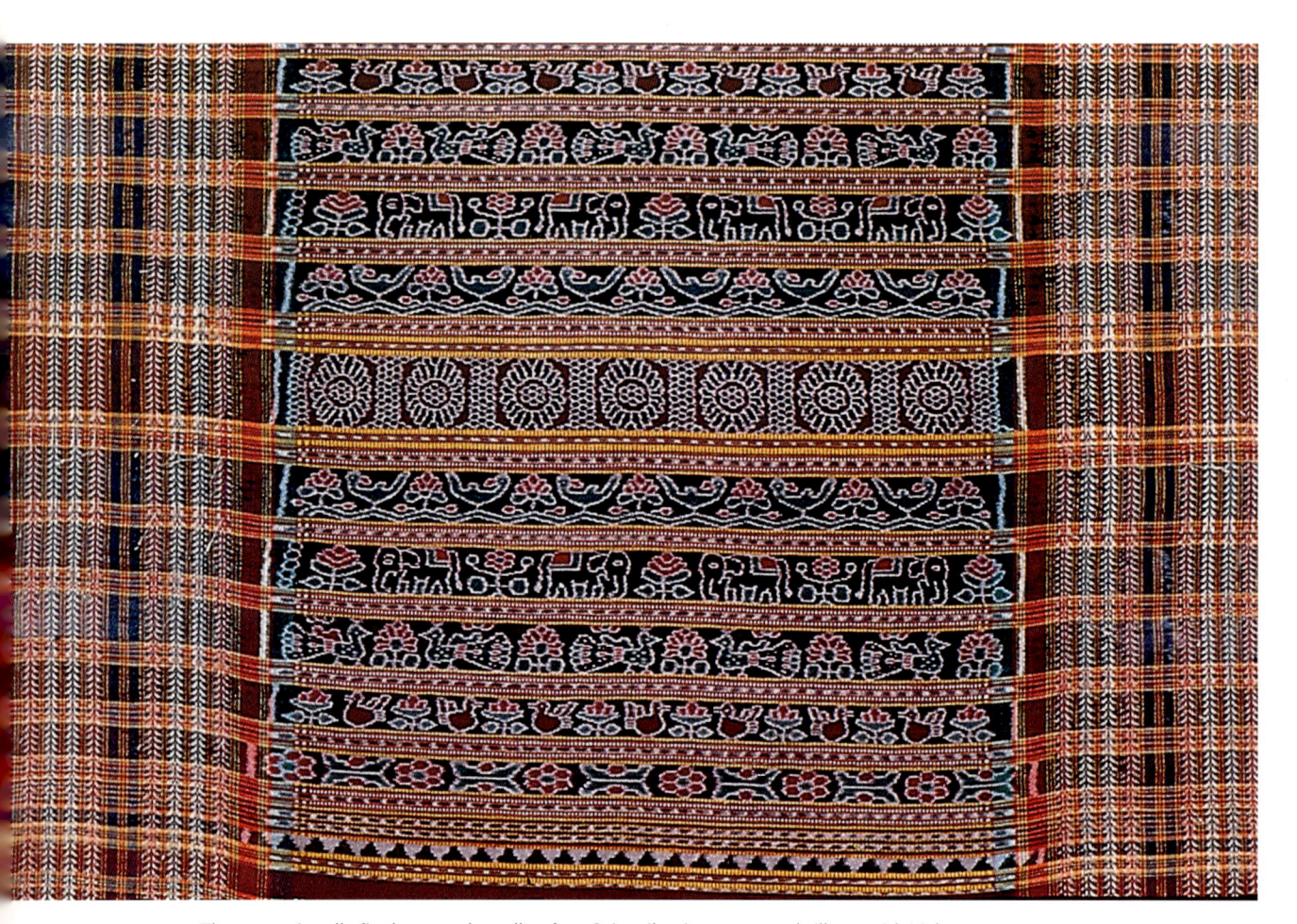

The exceptionally finely-wrought pallu of an Orissa ikat in cotton and silk, c. mid-19th century.

miniature paintings and antique manuscripts, using CAD (computer assisted design) to perfect the colour and design combination and match suitability of fabrics.

But computers were a far cry when the pioneer-activists of the earliest attempts, personalities like Kamaladevi Chattopadhyay, Pupul Jayakar and Rukmini Devi Arundale began their work. Kamaladevi was a close associate of Mahatma Gandhi and responsible for many of the earliest schemes in the field of crafts. Jasleen Dhamija, herself a distinguished textile scholar and author, recalls one such foray in the 'fifties when she accompanied Kamaladevi to Pochampalli in Andhra Pradesh in search of the weavers of the telia rumal: a heroic quest indeed!

> We set out at the crack of dawn in a jeep. It was a road used only by bullock carts; the jeep had to swing from side to side to manouevre ruts and avoid the cactus hedges on either side. With a wet towel on her head, her thick sari wrapped around her, she sat silent except to tell me: "I learnt from Bapu (Mahatma Gandhi) to keep a wet towel over my head in great heat."
> After a couple of hours we arrived at a tiny hamlet…I suddenly noticed blood trickling down her left arm — the cactus scratches had left their mark.
> The weavers clustered around and told us of not being paid enough for their work and not having a steady market. Kamaladevi then asked if they could weave a sari for there would be a good market for it. They hesitated. "No one will wear such thick saris! We have never made a continuous pattern. We will make mistakes, then who will pay for the warp?" Kamaladevi insisted that she would pay for the warp and that they would get twice the wages of the rumal for the sari.

The first three saris came one month later. A link was established and the weavers began to weave regularly, transferring their skills to household linen and yardage. Weavers were sent to Varanasi to learn silk weaving and introduced the silk ikat saris. After that is history. The demand grew so that other weaver villages, too, began to weave ikats. Not only Pochampalli but the entire district of Nalgonda prospered.

"Rocket" motif from Pochampalli.

END PIECE

Such were the voyages of discovery undertaken to seek out master craftsmen and traditional skills; they were inspired and suffused by the passion the early activists had for their task: the renaissance of excellence. The seekers sensed the vision of the craftsmen, and offered respect to that ancient knowledge that had been devalued for so long, close to dying out for lack of informed patronage. They ventured deep into interior areas in explorations for lost skills, hidden or half-forgotten under dusty, barely-used tools. In them was combined the missionary zeal for revival as well as a child-like curiosity for learning. Pride of class or status had no place here; and perhaps —because today we take for granted what they secured for us—we will never realise quite how much we owe to their quests, their documentation and their profound and compassionate understanding.

> *The Government is committed to providing a conducive environment to enable the Indian textile industry to realise its full potential, to achieve global excellence, and to fulfil its obligation to different sections of the society. In the fulfilment of these objectives, Government will enlist the co-operation and involvement of all stakeholders and ensure an effective and responsive delivery system.*
>
> National Textile Policy, 2000

The major thrust in the revival was, of course, the Government's, under whose aegis the pioneers worked, but there were many individuals and organisations who, over the years, played a vital part in areas of not only weaving but also block printing, tie-dye, embroidery and the revival of vegetable dyes. The biggest challenge was to make the

Calligraphy in ikat from Nuapatna, Orissa, represents a verse from the Gita Govinda and is meant to adorn the deities of the Jagannath temple in Puri.

products commercially viable by making them appealing to contemporary taste while encouraging traditional designs and skills. A number of success stories have been recorded. Using management and marketing skills yet with great sensitivity for the craftsmen, organisations turned near-moribund arts into thriving businesses, most of which are run as cooperatives.

Among the examples of such non-governmental organisations (NGOs) are the Rehwa Society of Maheshwar in Madhya Pradesh, where assistance with business basics and design inputs inspired looms into new action. Fashion designer Ritu Kumar can claim much of the credit for the recent nurturing and revival of the embroidery art of zardozi, where the craft was given new impetus by being used as embellishment for garments, bags and shawls. In different parts of India, individuals or groups have worked to preserve and protect traditional skills or designs or forms and give them new life: such as Suraiya Hussain in Hyderabad with her ikat, himroo, paithani and Machilipatnam kalamkari textiles; Laila Tyabji, who worked to make the chikan work of SEWA of Lucknow an embroidery success; Faith and John Singh of Anokhi in Jaipur in block printing, Satya Paul in screen printing; Shreela Debi in weaving from Bengal and many others. Much has been driven by the vast export market and its own particular demands.

Because of these combined efforts spread over so many years, today the handloom industry is the largest economic activity in the informal sector after agriculture, with approximately 3.5 million handlooms. Close to ten million people in rural areas depend on these looms fully or partly for their livelihood. Such figures make this a vast canvas but still the questions remain, the most basic one being of a sustained patronage which will ensure their future. Economies of scale simply cannot apply to works where both material and labour demand their right: the Patan patolas, the Paithans, the Benaras brocades, the temple saris, the Balucharis, all of which need discerning and sensitive buyers who have both taste and money, and also respect for the significance of the heritage. Patronage alone can assure the future of the industry, for only then will craftsmen pass on their skills to their children.

> *Life is like a piece of cloth being worked on the loom.*
> *Death is the weaver. And Night is the weft.*
> *As the weaver works the weft, he shortens the length that remains to be woven.*
> *Just as the passing of each night shortens the life of a man.*

Paraphrased from the Mukapanga Jataka

The fabric of heritage is so fragile, as we discover in so many areas from culture to ecology. Bits and pieces of living records vanish from day to day, a species there, a weave here, washed away as detritus from the unwanted, the obsolete. Nor is vitality immortal. A single earthquake, a flood, a typhoon, can wipe out so much, as we have seen; any one of these has the malignant power to erase centuries of crafts knowledge, skills that were absorbed in the womb. The spindles and needles, the looms, the printing blocks, the dye vats, bury themselves in sands or waters, and it will take effort — and, more than that, interest and commitment— to get them going again. Not just as museum pieces, or distress sales, or quaint village supplies to world fashion, but in the dignity of their own standing as expressions of skills that are proud and have meaning. And that are as real to us as any other part of our value system.

There can be no doubt, however, that it is crucial to all of us that this heritage remains part of our lives. As consumers, we too are "stakeholders" in this activity and thus responsible for its continuance. For over fifty centuries handcrafted textiles have been part of the rituals of our lives, our moments of passage marked by their beauty, their gravity, their colour. They are tangible symbols of inherited values and ancient skills, the loss of which would be irreparable to country and culture.

Select Bibliography

Historic Textiles of India at the Calico Museum, Calico Museum, Ahmedabad
    Vol 1, Indian Painted and Printed Fabrics, John Irwin & Margaret Hall
    Vol 2, Indian Embroideries, John Irwin & Margaret Hall
    Vol 3, Indian Pigment Paintings on Cloth, Kay Talwar & Kalyan Krishna
    Vol 4, Indian Tie-dyed Fabrics, Alfred Bühler, Eberhard Fischer, Marie-Louise Nabholz

Traditional Indian Textiles, John Gillow & Nicholas Barnard, Thames & Hudson, 1991

The Master Weavers, Pria Devi (ed) catalogue of the Festival of India in Britain, 1982

The Children of Barren Women, Pupul Jayakar, Penguin, 1994

The Glory of Indian Handicrafts, Kamaladevi Chattopadhyay, Indian Book Co., 1976

Textiles in Ancient India, Dr. Kiran Singh, Vishwa Vidayalaya Prakashan, 1994

Kalamkari, Nelly H. Sethna, Mapin Publishing, 1985

Crafts and Craftsmen in Traditional India, M. K. Pal, Kanak Publications, 1978

Homo Faber, Claude Alvares, Allied Publishers, 1979

National Handicrafts and Handlooms Museum, Jyotindra Jain & Aarti Aggarwala,
    Mapin Publishing, 1989